DATE DUE		

THE WAY PEOPLE LIVE

Life in Victorian England

Titles in The Way People Live series include:

Life Aboard the Space Shuttle
Life Along the Silk Road
Life Among the Aztec
Life Among the Ibo Women of Nigeria
Life Among the Inca
Life Among the Maya
Life Among the Samurai
Life During the American Revolution
Life During the Black Death
Life During the Crusades
Life During the Dust Bowl
Life During the Gold Rush
Life During the Great Depression
Life During the Middle Ages
Life During the Renaissance
Life During the Roaring Twenties
Life During the Russian Revolution
Life During the Spanish Inquisition
Life in a Japanese American Internment
    Camp
Life in a Medieval Castle
Life in a Medieval Monastery
Life in a Medieval Village
Life in a Nazi Concentration Camp
Life in a Wild West Show
Life in America During the 1960s
Life in an Amish Community
Life in Ancient Athens
Life in Ancient China

Life in Ancient Egypt
Life in Ancient Rome
Life in Berlin
Life in Castro's Cuba
Life in Communist Russia
Life in Elizabethan England
Life in Genghis Khan's Mongolia
Life in Hong Kong
Life in Moscow
Life in Tokyo
Life in the Australian Outback
Life in the Elizabethan Theater
Life in the Hitler Youth
Life in the Negro Baseball Leagues
Life in the North During the Civil War
Life in the South During the Civil War
Life of a Medieval Knight
Life of a Nazi Soldier
Life of a Roman Gladiator
Life of a Roman Soldier
Life of a Slave on a Southern
    Plantation
Life on Alcatraz
Life on Ellis Island
Life on an Everest Expedition
Life on the American Frontier
Life on the Oregon Trail
Life on the Pony Express
Life on the Underground Railroad

THE WAY PEOPLE LIVE

Life in Victorian England

by Duane C. Damon

LUCENT BOOKS

An imprint of Thomson Gale, a part of The Thomson Corporation

THOMSON

GALE

Detroit • New York • San Francisco • San Diego • New Haven, Conn. • Waterville, Maine • London • Munich

To my second family, Dan, Donna, Cara, and Sean,
and to the memory of Carita.

LIBRARY OF CONGRESS CATALOGING-IN-PUBLICATION DATA

Damon, Duane C.
  Life in Victorian England / by Duane C. Damon.
    p. cm. — (The way people live)
Includes bibliographical references and index.
Contents: Work and the lower classes—Work and the middle classes—The lower classes at home—Home for the middle and upper classes—Education in Victorian England—Social life and courtship—Victorians at leisure—Living, dying, and faith.
    ISBN 1-56006-391-2 (hard cover: alk. paper)
  1. Great Britain—Social life and customs—19th century—Juvenile literature. 2. Great Britain—History—Victoria, 1837–1901—Juvenile literature. I. Title. II. Series.

  DA533.D16 2005
  941.081—dc22

                                                                            2004030408

Printed in the United States of America

Contents

Discovering the Humanity in Us All

Books in The Way People Live series focus on groups of people in a wide variety of circumstances, settings, and time periods. Some books focus on different cultural groups, others on people in a particular historical time period, while others cover people involved in a specific event. Each book emphasizes the daily routines, personal and historical struggles, and achievements of people from all walks of life.

To really understand any culture, it is necessary to strip the mind of the common notions we hold about groups of people. These stereotypes are the archenemies of learning. It does not even matter whether the stereotypes are positive or negative; they are confining and tight. Removing them is a challenge that's not easily met, as anyone who has ever tried it will admit. Ideas that do not fit into the templates we create are unwelcome visitors—ones we would prefer remain quietly in a corner or forgotten room.

The cowboy of the Old West is a good example of such confining roles. The cowboy was courageous, yet soft-spoken. His time (it is always a he in our template) was spent alternatively saving a rancher's daughter from certain death on a runaway stagecoach or shooting it out with rustlers. At times, of course, he was likely to get a little crazy in town after a trail drive, but for the most part he was the epitome of inner strength. It is disconcerting to find out that the cowboy is human, even a bit childish. Can it really be true that cowboys would line up to help the cook on the trail drive grind coffee, just hoping he would give them a little stick of peppermint candy that came with the coffee shipment? The idea of tough cowboys vying with one another to help "Coosie" (as they called their cooks) for a bit of candy seems silly and out of place.

So is the vision of Eskimos playing video games and watching MTV, living in prefab housing in the Arctic. It just does not fit with what "Eskimo" means. We are far more comfortable with snow igloos and whale blubber, harpoons and kayaks.

Although the cultures dealt with in Lucent's The Way People Live series are often historically and socially well known, the emphasis is on the personal aspects of life. Groups of people, while unquestionably affected by their politics and their governmental structures, are more than those institutions. How do people in a particular time and place educate their children? What do they eat? And how do they build their houses? What kinds of work do they do? What kinds of games do they enjoy? The answers to these questions bring these cultures to life. People's lives are revealed in the particulars and only by knowing the particulars can we understand these cultures' will to survive and their moments of weakness and greatness.

This is not to say that understanding politics does not help to understand a culture. There is no question that the Warsaw ghetto, for example, was a culture that was brought about by the politics and social ideas of Adolf

Hitler and the Third Reich. But the Jews who were crowded together in the ghetto cannot be understood by the Reich's politics. Their life was a day-to-day battle for existence, and the creativity and methods they used to prolong their lives is a vital story of human perseverance that would be denied by focusing only on the institutions of Hitler's Germany. Knowing that children as young as five or six outwitted Nazi guards on a daily basis, that Jewish policemen helped the Germans control the ghetto, that children attended secret schools in the ghetto and even earned diplomas—these are the things that reveal the fabric of life, that can inspire, intrigue, and amaze.

Books in The Way People Live series allow both the casual reader and the student to see humans as victims, heroes, and onlookers. And although humans act in ways that can fill us with feelings of sorrow and revulsion, it is important to remember that "hero," "predator," and "victim" are dangerous terms. Heaping undue pity or praise on people reduces them to objects and strips them of their humanity.

Seeing the Jews of Warsaw only as victims is to deny their humanity. Seeing them only as they appear in surviving photos, staring at the camera with infinite sadness, is limiting, both to them and to those who want to understand them. To an object of pity the only appropriate response becomes "Those poor creatures!" and that reduces both the quality of their struggle and the depth of their despair. No one is served by such two-dimensional views of people and their cultures.

With this in mind, The Way People Live series strives to flesh out the traditional, two-dimensional views of people in various cultures and historical circumstances. Using a wide variety of primary quotations—the words not only of the politicians and government leaders but of the real people whose lives are being examined—each book in the series attempts to show an honest and complete picture of a culture removed from our own by time or space.

By examining cultures in this way, the reader not only will notice the glaring differences from his or her own culture but also will be struck by the similarities. For indeed, people share common needs—warmth, good company, stability, and affirmation from others. Ultimately, seeing how people really live, or have lived, can only enrich our understanding of ourselves.

The Nineteenth Century and Change

"We are living in an age of transition,"[1] observed a Victorian England social critic in 1858. For the millions of people inhabiting England during the reign of Queen Victoria (1837–1901), change was the hallmark of their times. Sooner or later, it touched the existence of Britons in almost every walk of life. It would affect their work, their standard of living, their social status, even their view of themselves. But such sweeping changes could not have come about without a powerful force to ignite them. That force was the Industrial Revolution.

Born in the mid-1700s, this turbulent era brought wave after wave of new inventions and scientific theories to the 1800s. New views on social and political issues inevitably followed these innovations. These changes in technology and thought had a profound impact on Britain. Victoria's era would witness the gradual death of its ancient agricultural way of life. In its place arose a dynamic new society based on laborsaving machines, urban living, and a blossoming middle class. This new society would also give the common man a bigger voice in government.

The Age of Steam and Industry

For two thousand years, technology had stood virtually still. Eighteenth-century Britons had little more mechanical help to do their work than the ancient Romans. People still built houses, plowed the land, prepared food, and made clothing using hand tools or basic animal-driven machines.

By the 1690s inventors were experimenting with steam engines as a means of powering machinery. Then in 1769 a Scottish instrument maker named James Watt devised an improved version of the crude steam engine already in use. His machine used hot steam and cool condensation to force pistons to move back and forth inside their cylinders. This action created the energy necessary to power the engine with less wasted steam. Building on Watt's success, inventors soon introduced boilers that could handle heavier kinds of work with higher-pressure steam. English and American inventors adapted steam engines to power full-sized riverboats and small-scale locomotives. The next step was to create bigger trains powerful enough to carry people. In 1825 British inventor George Stephenson opened the Stockton and Darlington Railway, the world's first passenger-bearing railroad.

The effect of the railways on British life was dramatic. In a remarkably short time, rail travel surpassed travel by foot, horseback, or coach. People who had never journeyed any farther than a few miles for work, shopping, or entertainment could now travel to nearly any destination in England in a matter of hours. Commerce was revolutionized. Powerful new trains could carry raw materials to factories with unheard-of speed. The finished products could then be transported from factories to local markets and seaports in less time than ever before. With the speed of moving goods steadily increasing, new and faster ways of producing those goods were needed.

For centuries, finished goods had been produced by workers and craftspeople working in their homes. A product might pass through the hands of several different laborers in separate locations before it was completed. Then, enterprising merchants hit on the idea of combining related tasks in a single location. They assembled a small number of workers in one shop and equipped them with the latest tools and equipment. Eventually factories, larger versions of the shops, began to spring up in urban areas like Birmingham, Manchester, and London. By centralizing production with laborsaving machines, manufacturers could turn out a higher volume of goods

Police stand at attention while huge crowds behind them cheer wildly during Queen Victoria's Diamond Jubilee procession through the streets of London.

at lower prices. Soon Britons were enjoying the highest standard of living in Europe.

The Class System

While the quality of life was moving upward, one English tradition remained unchanged—social position. In nineteenth-century England, class was everything. "Know your place" was the widely accepted attitude at every level of English society. Only two classes of society were traditionally recognized. The first was composed of aristocrats, people who owed their position to the land and titles they inherited. The second was made up of commoners, anyone who did not fit into the first class.

But there were more accurately *three* distinct divisions of Britons. The working classes, more than 70 percent of the population, supported themselves through physical labor, often dirty and sometimes dangerous. These classes included mine and factory workers, farm laborers, seamstresses, and domestic servants. The middle class (about 15 percent of the population in 1837 and 25 percent in 1901) encompassed the broadest spectrum of income levels and types of work. At one end, it embraced industrialists and wealthy bankers; the other end was composed of low-paid teachers and clerks. In between were physicians, clergymen, engineers, manufacturers, military officers, shopkeepers, and land-owning farmers.

The upper classes were made up of the landed gentry and the aristocracy, who comprised between 6 and 15 percent of the population. The gentry came by their wealth and land through their own efforts. In contrast, the aristocracy inherited their lands and wealth from their fathers. At the start of the era, these two groups held most of the wealth in England. They also held all the seats in Parliament, the national legislative body. But as the middle class grew in numbers and affluence, it also rose in social status and political power. That burgeoning power posed a clear threat to the prestige of the upper classes. Their growing uneasiness would only intensify in the decades following Victoria's ascension to the throne.

The Queen and Her Era

On June 20, 1837, the ailing King William IV passed away. Next in line for the English throne was his niece, the only child of his brother Edward, Duke of Kent. Eighteen-year-old Alexandrina Victoria had been raised and educated with an eye toward a future crown. On William's death, Victoria assumed her queenly role with dignity, a keen intelligence, and an abiding desire to serve her country well. She was officially crowned on June 28, 1838, in London's Westminster Abbey. She would remain queen for sixty-four years, the longest reign of any English monarch.

Queen Victoria's role in government was not so much to create laws as to rally public support for various issues. On a regular basis, Victoria signed documents, consulted with political figures, and offered her own views on this issue or that. But many of her royal responsibilities were ceremonial, not official. Throughout her reign, Parliament wielded the greatest political power in England. Yet even that great body was not immune to change. As the decades passed, Parliament grudgingly granted more and more political influence to the middle and working classes. Power in England was no longer to be held exclusively in the hands of the high-born and the wealthy.

For her part, the queen sought to set a moral tone for her people. Less than three advisor to the queen, and oversaw programs for the arts, agriculture, industry, and sciences. In the home, Albert was as devoted to his marriage and his children as Victoria. Eventually they produced nine offspring. The obvious joy and affection that the royal couple brought to their family life made them a role model for all England.

England and the World

But the world outside the palace walls was not nearly so placid. Social unrest and economic problems dominated the 1830s and 1840s. The Corn Laws heavily taxed imported grains like wheat, barley, oats, and corn, raising the cost of bread and other foods. Workers suffered through long hours, unsafe labor conditions, and low wages. As the factory system flourished, falling prices forced the layoffs of thousands of employees. Workers rebelled and rioted in 1831 and 1832. To appease them, Parliament passed the Reform Act of 1832, granting a limited number of men the right to vote. Further reforms began to improve working conditions and ease the plight of the poor. In 1839 the Chartist movement created the People's Charter, which demanded further political changes. While the initial effort failed, the movement sparked a new wave of political, social, and economic activism.

The 1840s through the 1870s saw slow but tangible progress. Parliament passed laws to improve education and make it more accessible. Bills to better protect children at work and at home were enacted. Food was made

In 1840 Queen Victoria and Prince Albert, the queen's first cousin, were wed.

years after taking the throne, Victoria married her German-born first cousin, Albert, Prince of Saxe-Coburg-Gotha. It was a rarity among royal marriages—a genuine love match. Intelligent and farsighted, Albert served as private secretary and confidential

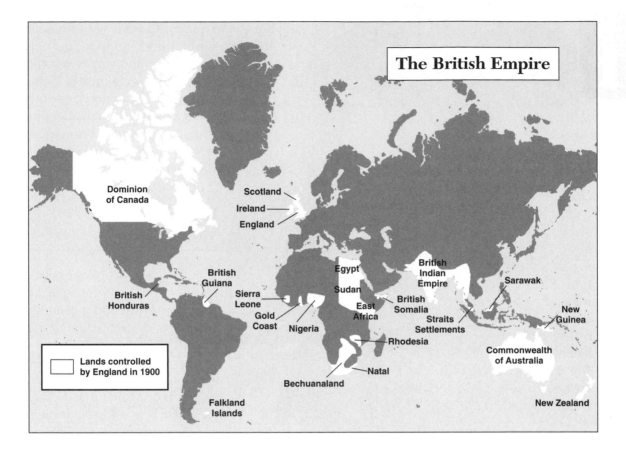

The British Empire

Dominion
of Canada

Scotland

Ireland

England

British
Guiana

British
Honduras

Sierra
Leone

Gold
Coast

Nigeria

Egypt

Sudan

East
Africa

British
Indian
Empire

Sarawak

British
Somalia

Straits
Settlements

New
Guinea

Rhodesia

Commonwealth
of Australia

Bechuanaland

Natal

Lands controlled
by England in 1900

Falkland
Islands

New Zealand

more sanitary; housing became safer. Workers were allowed to join labor unions. While women were still denied the vote, they nevertheless advanced in their right to own property, receive an education, and hold a job.

Meanwhile, the wealth and power of England made the country the envy of the world. Eager to acquire new lands to expand trade, Britain, as well as the United States and other developed nations, seized and colonized sections of other countries throughout the 1800s. At midcentury, Britain already controlled Canada and India. The final quarter of the century witnessed an incredible expansion of the British Empire. In that time, England gained 4.7 million square miles (12.2 million sq. km) of territory in China, Australia, New Zealand, Burma, Borneo, the

West Indies, Africa, and many other regions. To govern and police those territories took a huge navy, and a strong and mobile army. Much of England's time, men, and resources were consumed in fighting wars and revolts in India, Afghanistan, and other locations just to maintain control.

Yet Englishmen took pride in their great foreign holdings. They were fond of the expression, "The sun never sets on the British Empire."[2] They were pleased by their reputation as "Workshop of the World."[3] They were aware that they were in the midst of a period of great change, but were confident they could meet it head-on. As early as 1851, they gave a name to this era, one that reflected both their national pride and their devotion to their monarch. They called themselves Victorians.

CHAPTER 1

"The Darkest Shadow:" Work and the Lower Classes

In Victoria's era as much as any other, the work people performed did much to define their lifestyle and status. A Victorian's employment was a sort of badge of his or her station in life. The low status accorded to the low-paid working classes, however, was in some ways softened by the work ethic of the time. Some thinkers of the period even saw a religious quality in labor. "All true Work is sacred," wrote the social critic Thomas Carlyle in 1843. "In all true Work, were it but true hand-labor, there is something of divineness."[4] But divine or not, the working lives of the lower classes in nineteenth-century England remained a grim, day-to-day battle to exist.

It was not only the adults who labored hard and earned little. By the thousands, children also put in long hours on farms, in factories, in mines, or on the streets. In city or country, the pay was pathetically low and the conditions often horrific. "Perhaps the darkest shadow to have fallen over the nineteenth century was the harsh and often inhumane treatment of Britain's laboring classes," historian Kristine Hughes observes, "and especially of the women and children who made up so many of its numbers."[5]

Country Labor

Agriculture was England's oldest industry. In the farmlands of Yorkshire, Sussex, Lancashire, and elsewhere, Victorian laborers were descended from peasants who had worked the same fields in the Middle Ages. In 1851 alone, nearly 2 million workers out of a population of 21 million made their living from the soil. Of that number, nearly 11 percent were women. The crops they harvested and the animals they raised formed the cornerstone of the British food supply. As political scientist Daniel Pool explains,

> The three great products of English farming in the 1800s were corn, sheep, and cattle. "Corn" as the English used the word was not the American corn of corn on the cob . . . but rather referred to grains such as wheat, barley, and oats. Wheat was grown to make bread, barley to make beer and ale (and sometimes bread), and oats to make oatcakes and other food as well as feed for horses. Cattle provided meat, butter, and milk and pulled plows and farm wagons.[6]

British farming was conducted at three different levels. "The gentry owned the land, the farmers rented it, the laborers worked it,"[7] historian W.J. Reader summarizes. At the top of this hierarchy sat the landowners. These were either aristocrats, men of noble birth, or the gentry, wealthy men from the upper middle classes who had purchased sizable tracts of land. From the landowner, the tenant farmer rented parcels of land, usually 100 acres (40.5ha) or less, to be cultivated. In turn, the tenant farmer hired laborers from the surrounding areas to work the fields and

SCOTLAND

North Atlantic Ocean

Dundee

Glasgow Edinburgh

North Sea

Newcastle
Sunderland
Darlington
York
Leeds
Hull
Manchester
Liverpool Sheffield
Stoke Nottingham
Derby
Norwich

Irish Sea

Dublin

IRELAND

WALES ENGLAND
Birmingham Oxford
Newport
Cardiff London
Swansea Bristol
Southampton
Exeter Portsmouth

★ Capital
● City

ENGLAND

In the 1850s, the average wage for an adult male was only 11 shillings a week, well short of the minimum 15 or 16 shillings he needed weekly to support his family. (A shilling was worth 1/20 of the British pound, which was valued at around $4.90 in U.S. currency at that time. In the year 2000, the pound was valued at $1.52.) If the worker was fortunate, the farmer who employed him might throw in a shabby one- or two-room cottage either for free or a reduced rent. This included a small plot outside the cottage to grow vegetables or keep chickens or a pig. Occasionally the farmer might even reward his workers, or "cottagers," with a ration of milk, bacon, and potatoes. At harvest time, this ration included beer. With these extras, and good farming weather, a cottager family might barely make it through the year. Without them, it faced starvation.

tend his livestock. The laborer occupied a bleak rung on the agricultural ladder —the bottom. "The agricultural laborer was not a romantic figure," historical writer Gillian Avery explains. "He was seen . . . as a shambling, slouching, boorish, degraded creature, improvident [not thrifty], reckless, and always on the watch for what he could get out of the gentry."[8]

Laborers could expect little in life beyond an arduous present and a bleak future. Their toil was hard and their pay inadequate.

Daily Toil, Daily Bread

Running a farm required a variety of back-breaking tasks. Men and sometimes women plowed, planted, weeded, hoed, dug ditches, mended fences, tended animals, and brought in the harvest. Few machines were available to ease their labor. The basic tools at their disposal included steel-bladed plows, axes, hoes, spades, pitchforks (for tossing hay or straw from one spot to another), scythes (a sharp, curved blade for cutting stalks of grain), and flails (a two-pieced wooden tool for threshing). While working, laborers generally wore a simple loose-fitting smock that reached nearly to the knees or, in the case of children, nearly to the feet. The average worker put in at least fourteen hours a day in the fields, plus a walk of several miles to and from work.

While men performed the hardest labor, their wives often carried a load nearly as heavy. Reader relates this example:

A woman of 1850 said she had had 13 children, of whom seven grew up, and she had been accustomed to field work for 11 hours a day at haytime and harvest. In the autumn she would go out gleaning [gathering grain left behind by reapers], perhaps from two in the morning to seven in the evening, perhaps as much as seven miles from home, and she would take three daughters (aged 10, 15 and 18) with her. For this effort, she would reckon six bushels of corn a very good reward. [9]

During the final quarter of the 1800s, females did less of the regular field labor than they had earlier in the century. Yet there was still plenty to do, as Kristine Hughes points out:

While women were often hired temporarily at harvest times, they also worked full time at potato gathering, turnip pulling, weeding, hoeing, binding hop [a plant used in brewing beer], and all manner of vegetable and fruit picking. Often, their children worked alongside them, and it was not unusual for

After a grueling day of picking hops, a team of farmworkers in Victorian England empties their harvest into a large container.

employers to advertise for entire families of farmworkers.[10]

Youngsters performed other tasks, too. In the fields, they picked stones out of newly turned earth or frightened birds away from freshly sown corn. At other times, children were required to pull weeds, clean turnips, and later, to guide horses and herd sheep or goats. As exhausting as farm labor could be, it was still better than the alternatives. "When I am not at work I do not often get bread and meat for dinner," one boy declared. "I had rather work than play; you get [the] most victuals [food] when you work."[11]

"A Hole in the Black Earth"

While farmworkers toiled above ground, far below them other Britons labored in darkness and danger. Miners worked in dark, narrow shafts many feet below the ground, in air that was thin with heat and foul with coal dust. Their job was to dig or chip the coal out of rocky walls, collect it, and haul it up to ground level.

"A coal mine," declared the novelist D.H. Lawrence on a 1926 visit to his hometown of Eastwood, "remains a hole in the black earth, where blackened men hew and shovel and sweat."[12] Lawrence had reason to retain distinct memories of Eastwood from his boyhood in the 1880s. His uncle James had been killed in a mining accident in nearby Brinsley, and his father had been physically ruined by decades of underground labor.

The hardships endured by the hundreds of thousands of workers in England's coal mines were many. Social historian J.F.C. Harrison paints a grim picture:

At the coal face the "hewers" [workers assigned to break the rock], naked and on their knees, hacked away at the coal with their picks. In narrow seams, which could be as low as two feet, three inches in parts of the Yorkshire coal-fields, the face worker had to lie on his side, use his elbow as a lever, and pick away at the coal. Behind him the "hurriers" [those who retrieved the coal] dragged away the cut coal in wheelless tubs or small trucks to the pit bottom, where it was hoisted to the surface or . . . carried up ladders in corves [baskets].[13]

A workday for miners was twelve hours or longer. Picks, shovels, and their own muscles were their only tools, a flickering candle or a dim safety lamp their only light. These were scant protection against the countless perils facing them daily. Author Jeffrey Meyers describes those perils:

The men might be crushed or buried alive by a sudden fall of earth that blocked their way out of the mine. The deep pits might suddenly be inundated with floods or choked with poison gas and firedamp [a combustible gas, mostly methane, occurring naturally in coal mines]. The miners' lungs were clogged with dust as they breathed the odors of stinking horses and sweating men. . . . The mines were always dark, dirty and dusty as well as hot, wet and cramped. Eating, drinking, urinating and defecating all took place in a confining space, and rats ran through the stagnant water.[14]

Under these conditions, nearly one thousand miners died every year in mining accidents. By the age of forty, most survivors were afflicted with an inflammation of the lungs called "black spittle," contracted by breathing in coal dust. Arthritis crippled many others. Hoping to compensate for these risks, mining

"The King of Laborers": The Navvy

The coming of the railroad in the 1830s and 1840s brought an immense burst of construction. To lay the thousands of miles of track required by the "iron horse," the land first needed to be dug out and shaped. The tough, hardened men who performed this massive task were called "navvies," after the canal builders, or "navigators," of the 1700s. There were two hundred thousand navvies in 1845 alone.

Across England, armies of navvies were hired to blaze trails through rocks and hills, around peaks, and along slopes. The work had to be precise; train travel demanded gently rising grades and carefully banked turns. When bridges were required, navvies helped construct those too. In *The Early Victorians*, J.F.C. Harrison says that the work

"was extremely hard and often dangerous. A navvy was expected to shovel about 20 tons of earth and rock a day on the basic jobs of cutting, banking, and tunneling. Excavating was done with pick and shovel, the navvies working in rows. . . . Wet weather frequently created slippery, and therefore dangerous conditions. The earth from the bottom of a cutting [a a channel dug through high ground], for instance, had to be taken out in barrows hauled up the steep sides of the cutting, and it was easy to slip and fall beneath the overturned barrow-load of muck. Tunnels were nearly always deep in mud, and in addition there was the danger hazard of the crude methods of blasting [using explosives to shatter rock walls]."

The navvy's lifestyle was rough and unsettled. Because he roved from one job to the next, a permanent home or marriage was out of the question. He filled his free time with heavy eating, hard drinking, and brawling. Yet his special abilities commanded respect. "The popular image of the navvy as a violent, godless, drunken fellow, far removed from the 'refining' influences of home and family, contained much truth," Harrison adds. "At the same time it had to be admitted that the navvy was 'the king of laborers'."

companies offered workers better wages and free housing. Yet these were not much incentive; most worked in the mines because they had little choice.

Children of the Earth

Despite its hazards, coal mining employed women and children as well as men. The 1841 census counted more than 2,000 female miners out of 118,000 in Great Britain. Their tasks were nearly as physically demanding as those of the men. Working as "putters," women were strapped into crude harnesses equipped with a chain attached to coal-laden trucks (small wheeled carts). Their job was to drag the freshly cut coal out from the coal face to cagelike lifts for removal from the shaft. The experience was described in the early 1840s by a Lancashire woman:

I have a belt round my waist and a chain passing between my legs, and I go on my hands and feet. The water comes up to clog [shoe] tops, and I have seen it over my thighs. I have drawn [pulled a truck] till I have the skin off me. The belt and

English coal miners use a pick, hammer, and chisel to hew coal from a mine, while other miners prepare to yoke a cartload of coal to a horse.

chain is worse when we are in the family way [pregnant].[15]

Juvenile mine workers fared no better. While most boys and girls went to work underground by the age of twelve or fourteen, some began as early as five. Because of their smaller size, the youngest ones could squeeze into seams and cavities older children could not. These youngsters often served as "trappers," entering the pits early in the morning to open and close ventilator doors that controlled airflow through the shaft. Twelve to fourteen hours later, they were the last to leave.

The plight of child miners eventually attracted official attention. Over time, government inquiries led to such badly needed reforms as shorter hours and safer working conditions. Yet many mine owners were slow to make improvements that cut into their profits.

At Work in the City: The Factories

By the 1830s and 1840s, legions of mine workers, tired of dangerous conditions underground, were deserting the mines. Joining this exodus were farm laborers driven from the countryside by poor harvests and general dissatisfaction. Their destination was the factories and mills of England's burgeoning industrial centers. In Manchester, Birmingham, Sheffield, and other cities, the machines of the Industrial Revolution were changing the nature of work for hundreds of thousands of Britons.

Work in the factories and mills was less physically demanding than farming or mining, and working indoors protected laborers from bad weather. Yet factory work posed substantial dangers of its own. Since production workers were trained to perform the same task over and over, the repetitive movements of hands, arms, elbows, and shoulders often resulted in gradual injury. The very act of breathing carried risk. In textile mills, giant power looms spat out clouds of cotton dust. In iron and steel factories, machines for shaping metal spewed tiny fragments into the air. Match-making plants exposed workers to phosphorus contamination, which attacked the jaw and teeth. Pottery plants produced dangerous levels of lead. The excessive heat of foundries (metalworking plants with huge furnaces) and the constant, deafening roar of heavy machinery were two more perils of factory labor.

Always present was the danger of physical injury or death while operating large, powerful machines. In the event of mishaps, workers could expect little sympathy from factory owners. The report of the Committee on Factory Children's Labor 1831–1832 included an interview with Samuel Coulson, whose oldest daughter was injured in a textile mill:

Interviewer: Had any of [your children] any accident in consequence of this labor?

Coulson: Yes, my eldest daughter when she went first there. She had been there about five weeks, and used to fettle [tend] the frames when they were running, and my eldest girl agreed with one of the others to fettle hers that time. . . . While she was learning more about the work, the overlooker came by and said, "Ann, what are you doing there?" She said, "I am doing it for my companion, in order that I may know more about it." He said, "Let go, drop it this minute," and the cog caught her forefinger nail, and screwed it off below the knuckle, and she was five weeks in Leeds Infirmary.

Interviewer: Has she lost that finger?

Coulson: It is cut off at the second joint.

Interviewer: Were her wages paid during that time?

Coulson: As soon as the accident happened the wages were totally stopped. [16]

Many accidents involving machinery were far worse than losing part of a finger. Levers, gears, and rollers crushed hands, mangled arms, and even killed their operators. In time, reform laws reduced the number of children eligible for factory labor, and more women were hired to fill in the gaps. Either way, it was a bargain for factory owners: Women as well as children worked for a fraction of the wages paid to men.

At Work in the City: The Streets

As thousands of displaced workers poured into urban areas, towns and cities became more crowded. Good jobs became more difficult to find, and decent housing more scarce. Many new city dwellers found themselves among the ranks of the urban working poor. Sociologist Henry Mayhew and his researchers conducted a broad study of the laboring class in the 1840s and 1850s. They defined this group as "all that large class who live by either selling, showing, or doing something through the country . . . street folk —street-sellers, street-buyers, street-finders, street performers, street artisans or working peddlers and street laborers." [17]

The prospect of making a living, even a poor one, as a street vendor was made possible

"No Slavery Is Worse": The Dressmaker

They sewed sleeves and hemmed skirts. They stitched petticoats and attached buttons. They toiled grueling hours with needle, thread, and scissors in cramped rooms and in half darkness. "They" were a segment of the British female workforce seldom seen and often forgotten by the public: the dressmaker.

In 1841 the number of women and girls employed in dressmaking and millinery (the making and decorating of hats and caps) passed 106,000. Many of the girls came from rural areas, while others were the daughters of lower-middle-class parents fallen on hard times. To learn the business, many girls paid a stiff premium for a two- or three-year apprenticeship to the shopowner.

Some considered dressmaking to be a step up socially from factory labor. Yet government investigations in the 1840s revealed conditions in a dressmaker's shop to be worse than those in cotton mills. Mill-

iners and dressmakers commonly put in sixteen-hour days, five or six days a week. During London's two social seasons, they might labor from 4:00 A.M. to midnight to meet the demand for new dresses and hats. This meant long hours bent over a garment doing close needlework by the light of a single candle. This kind of prolonged punishment damaged both the back and the eyes. In one instance, "A girl of seventeen," Wanda F. Neff reports in *Victorian Working Women: An Historical and Literary Study of Women in British Industries and Professions, 1832–1850,* "on account of an order for general mourning, did not change her dress for nine days or nights. She rested on a mattress on the floor; her food was cut up and placed beside her so that she could sew while she ate. As a result, she lost her sight." This sort of hardship prompted one witness to declare, "No slavery is worse than that of the dressmaker's life in London."

by the absence of electricity. Lacking refrigeration, households found it necessary to purchase food and supplies on a daily basis. The routine began around 8:00 A.M., when bakers and milkmaids first appeared on the streets. Shouting "Hot loaves!" and ringing their bells, bread vendors hawked their wares to waiting customers. Fresh warm rolls sold for one or two for a penny, and in winter crumpets and muffins were available. Meanwhile, a group of young women, up since 4:30 or 5:00 A.M., had begun their day by milking their cows and pouring the milk into clean dairy cans. Then they set out on their regular delivery routes, returning by noon to rewash the cans and milk the cows a second time.

Shortly after the bakers and milkmaids hit the street, other vendors appeared.

Women offered baked or boiled apples from their barrows (wooden wheelbarrow-style carts), using glowing coals to keep the fruit hot. Ragged youngsters sold live rabbits from crude cages. Men toted bandboxes (rounded containers for storing small items of apparel) on the end of a pole that rests on the shoulder. Other vendors sold dog and cat food made from horse meat, young bull livers, or the stomach linings of cattle. Flower girls retrieved blossoms left over from sales in the Covent Garden markets and assembled small bunches of flowers to sell as "buttonholes."

While these products were popular, prepared food remained the most sought-after item. From barrows positioned along the streets, vendors sold fried fish, kidney puddings, oysters, pickled whelks (large, edible marine snails), hot eels, mutton, and sheep's trotters (feet). Other popular choices were walnuts, roasted chestnuts, oranges, ginger beer, and a cold concoction called hokey-pokey, known today as ice cream. Author Nicolas Bentley reports,

> Coffee stalls did a brisk trade all day in food as well as drinks. In 1842 there were some 300 in London selling, besides coffee, tea and cocoa at a penny a mug . . . ham sandwiches, watercress, boiled eggs, baked potatoes, and slices of cake or bread and butter. Nothing cost more than twopence [roughly one U.S. cent] and a filling if not particularly nourishing meal could be got for sixpence.[18]

Roving tradesmen offered various services such as knife sharpening, fixing the woven

Londoners line up to buy ice cream from a street vendor. Street vending was a common occupation in Victorian London.

In this 1877 photo, a chimney sweep poses with his brushes and chummy, the small boy who climbed inside the chimneys and cleaned them.

Chimney Sweeps and "Chummies"

The lives of those who spent their working hours in the cramped and sooty darkness of chimney flues made one more tragic chapter in the story of the Victorian lower working class. Small children were often forced to assist adult chimney sweeps in their hazardous and filthy work. As author Kristine Hughes describes it in *The Writer's Guide to Everyday Life in Regency and Victorian England: From 1811–1901*: "In the poorer districts across England, where children were plentiful and wages low, children of any age from four upward were sold to master sweeps, who were under no obligation to look after them, physically or morally." These youthful workers were called "climbing boys" or "chummies." Their great value to the chimney sweeps lay in their small size.

"Children as young as four or five were sent crawling up the 12-by-14-inch chimneys (some were only seven inches square) of nice middle class homes to clean out some of the five bushels of soot that coal fires deposited there on the average each year," writes Daniel Pool in *What Jane Austen Ate and Charles Dickens Knew*. "Since the chimney surfaces were generally smooth inside, only the pressure of their elbow and knees got—or kept—the small boys up, and older boys often stood below them holding lighted straws to their feet or sticking them with pins to 'encourage' them. Or they were simply beaten."

Injuries and even deaths were commonplace in the lives of the "chummies." It was all too easy for a child to get lost in the often twisting, soot-coated system of flues built into many chimneys. He could become jammed inside its narrow passages and suffocate to death, or he could be seriously burned when a fire was lighted in the fireplace while he was inside. Some chummies continued to work even after suffering repeated injuries on the job. Although the government enacted laws in both 1840 and 1864 to outlaw this kind of labor, it was many years before the practice came to an end.

seats of chairs, and chimney sweeping. The foulness left on city streets by horse-drawn traffic created yet another service, one simple enough for children to perform. Equipped with homemade brooms, crossing sweepers received small tips in exchange for clearing a path for well-dressed ladies and gentlemen. Yet not all these workers were youngsters, as Mayhew's interview with a deaf, eighty-year-old widow shows:

I goes every morning, winter or summer, frost or snow; and at the same hour (five o'clock); people certainly don't think of giving so much [in payment] in fine weather. Nobody ever mislested [molested] me, and I never mislested nobody. If they gives me a penny, I thanks 'em; and if they give me nothing, I thanks 'em all the same.[19]

Domestic Service

But work on the streets could be difficult and uncertain. To avoid it, many Britons chose to work in the homes of other people. Domestic service was the second-largest type of employment in Victorian England. It was the largest for girls and women. In 1851 alone, at least 1 million people, more than 13 percent of the working population, had jobs "in service."

By 1890 one-third of working females between the ages of fifteen and twenty made their living this way.

Most domestic servants were female. In urban townhouses and country estates, they worked as cooks, housekeepers, ladies' maids, parlor maids, scullery maids, dairy maids, nursery maids, washerwomen, and char-women. Their typical uniform was a simple dress of some printed or striped fabric, partially covered by a plain, full-length apron and topped by a white cap. During the afternoons and evenings, serving women usually wore a black dress with a more elaborate apron and cap. Men entering service found positions as valets, footmen, pages, hall porters, coach-men, grooms (who cared for horses), boot boys, or gardeners. Their uniforms were coordinating jackets and trousers called livery. Like the cook and the housekeeper, the position of butler was held by someone with many years of service behind him.

Working-class girls soon discovered advantages to working in the homes of their "betters." For one thing, the food and living conditions were better than they had been at home. Thrifty employees could save money because room and board were furnished by their employers. And the increased contact with tradesmen, apprentices, and male servants improved their chances of meeting a suitable husband.

"On My Knees"

Inevitably, there were drawbacks to domestic service. "Their work was in no sense as arduous as that of industrial or outdoor laborers," Harrison has commented, "but it was continual, tiring and often monotonous."[20] For example, the duties of the housemaid—dusting, sweeping, and general cleaning—were physical and required no real skills. She might also carry water upstairs, draw baths, and empty slops (buckets or basins containing human waste). In homes without male servants, the housemaid might also carry coals and tend fires.

A typical day in the life of a household laborer is illustrated by the diary entry for July 14, 1860 of Victorian maidservant Hannah Cullwick:

> Opened the shutters & lighted the kitchen fire. . . . Swept & dusted the rooms & the hall. Laid the hearth & got breakfast up. Clean'd 2 pairs of boots. Made the beds & emptied the slops. Clean'd & wash'd the breakfast things up. Clean'd the plate; clean'd the knives & got dinner up. . . . Clean'd the kitchen up; unpacked a hamper. Took 2 chickens to Mrs. Brewer's & brought the message back. Made a tart & pick'd & gutted 2 ducks & roasted them. . . . Clean'd the pantry on my knees & scour'd the tables. Scrubbed the flags around the house & clean'd the window sills. Got tea at 9 for the master & Mrs. Warwick. . . . Clean'd the privy & passage & scullery floor on my knees. Wash'd the dog & clean'd the sinks down. Put the supper ready for Ann to take up, for I was too dirty & tired to go upstairs. Wash'd in a bath & to bed.[21]

Domestic service offered a few opportunities for advancement. A scullery maid might in time move up from scrubbing floors to the position of kitchen maid. From there she might rise to cook. Around the age of twelve, a lad might enter a household as a page boy. A page boy's duties consisted of running errands and cleaning the shoes of employers and staff. This work prepared him for the position of footman, with a broader range of

Domestic servants of a Victorian household pose with their cleaning implements in this 1885 photo.

tasks: delivering messages, answering the door, tending fires, cleaning silverware, and escorting his employers on business or shopping trips. Eventually he might set his sights on a butler's position, a job paying two or three times that of his own.

Like farm laborers, coal miners, factory workers, and street vendors, British domestic servants still occupied the lowest class in Victorian society. Significantly, the working class was also the country's largest class. As it had for centuries, England's greatest wealth rested with the smallest class, the aristocrats and landed gentry. But during the reign of Victoria, a great social and economic shift was beginning. The best hope of the working class lay in moving up to the next level on the social pyramid—the middle class.

"Seize the Prizes:" Work and the Middle Classes

The group of Victorians most deeply affected by the Industrial Revolution was the middle class. The explosion of technology resulting from the revolution spawned a multitude of new manufacturing possibilities and expanded England's international trade. Most importantly for middle class Britons, the new technology also created a host of new jobs. Workers of the lowest classes were often too unschooled or too oppressed to take advantage of the new occupations. The upper classes largely ignored the growing opportunities in business and trade, fields they felt were beneath them. The changes provided those in the middle, however, with a long-awaited chance to improve their lifestyle and raise their social status.

A Broad Spectrum

"The middle classes were the great success story of the Victorian age," historians Hilary Evans and Mary Evans have observed. "They created the conventions of the age—and followed them. They forged its values—and lived by them."[22]

Central to these values was hard work. This was not because labor was in itself a noble endeavor, but because it was the straightest path to success. For the middle classes of Victoria's time, the time-honored social order was no longer acceptable. "They found a society in which most of the best things in life—wealth, property, social position—were conventionally regarded as belonging to those who were 'born to them,'" writes Reader. "They wanted to substitute for it a society in which those who had the ability might seize the prizes."[23]

The middle classes applied their abilities to an immense range of occupations and professions. From lowly clerks to rich industrialists, and shopkeepers to doctors, middle-class workers were a varied group. Teachers, seamstresses, and policemen were among those who fell into the lower-middle-class category. Occupations such as military officers, low-ranking government employees, and store owners made up the center of the middle class.

Enjoying the highest social standing in the middle class were the professionals, also known as the upper-middle-class. University professors, Church of England clergymen, lawyers and physicians, and high-level government workers were all members of this group. As the century wore on, civil engineers, architects, and bankers also joined the professional class. But respectability was slower in coming to the fields of trade and manufacturing. Because they had long been associated with labor performed by hand, these occupations were considered unsuitable for gentlemen.

The Lower Middle Class

Lower-middle-class workers liked to believe themselves a step above the working class. In their less physical occupations, they were not likely to strain their backs or dirty their hands. But in many cases their positions were only a very small step up. They often labored in excess of fourteen hours per day with little or no compensation for overtime.

Such was the lot of the men and women who worked in retail shops. The typical Victorian business establishment was small, usually owned by one person or a small partnership. Only a few clerks were needed to keep the business going, and those were generally male, as were the apprentices, who paid the shop owner premiums to learn his trade and ensure their own futures. In the early 1880s, future author H.G. Wells was employed as an assistant in a draper's (cloth seller's) shop in Southsea. In his autobiography, he recalls being awakened with his fellow apprentices at seven A.M. to prepare for the day:

> [We] were down in the shop in a quarter of an hour, to clean windows, unwrapper goods and fixtures, [and] dust, generally before eight. At eight we rushed upstairs to get first go at the wash basins, dressed for the day and at half past eight partook of a bread and butter breakfast before descending again. Then came window

Young middle-class Englishmen at an army training school engage in various leisure activities, including reading, cards, and billiards.

The Shopkeeper

The owner of a Victorian shop occupied a higher rung on the middle-class ladder than his assistants and apprentices. After all, he assumed the responsibility for not only the success of his enterprise, but the well-being of his family and employees. The daily environment of one such shopkeeper is reflected in these recollections of his daughter, published in the October 10, 1961, issue of the London *Times*:

"It must have been in 1890 that we went to live 'over the shop.' . . . Below, in the basement, was a huge kitchen, with cellars behind where some of the pledges [items pawned for money in hopes of redeeming them later] were stored—not very interesting ones, we thought—fenders, fire-irons, tool-boxes, spades, and the like. On the ground floor was the shop, a long narrow place, everlasting gaslit and festooned with unredeemed pledges of all kinds, where Dad, with two assistants and two or three apprentices, carried on his business of pawnbroker and jeweler. On the first floor were the family sitting-room and bedrooms, and above, in the attics, were two warehouses, one for clothing and the other—a fascinating place to us—for ornaments, curios, and musical instruments. . . . The shop itself we saw less of. . . . From Monday to Friday it was open from 8 A.M. until 8 P.M. and on Saturdays it never closed before 11 P.M. . . . The apprentices . . . were almost part of the family, having a hasty dinner with us in the kitchen, still in their shirtsleeves and shiny black aprons, between spells of 'watching the shop,' for there was no midday closing then.

The shop had two entrances, one leading to the sales counter, which was open, and the other to the pledge counter, which was divided off by partitions so that shy customers could not see one another. At one end of the pledge counter was a desk where one of the assistants made out pawn tickets in duplicate, one ticket for the client and the other for an apprentice to pin or stick to the pledge, and entered each transaction in a huge ledger."

dressing [decorating with merchandise] and dressing out [setting up displays] in the shop. I had to fetch goods for the window dresser and arrange patterns or pieces of fabric on the brass line above the counter. Every day or so the costume window had to be arranged, and I had to go in the costume room and fetch [the mannequins] and carry them the length of the shop to the window dresser. . . .

Half an hour before closing time we began to put away for the last time and "wrapper up" [prepare to close the shop]. . . . As soon as the doors were shut and the last customer gone, the assistants departed and we junior apprentices rushed from behind counters, scattered wet sawdust out of pails over the floor and swept it up again with great zest and speed, the last rite of the day. By half past eight we were upstairs and free, supping on bread and butter, cheese and small [weak, inexpensive] beer.[24]

Men in Uniform

For young men with a yen for the sea—or a history of trouble in school or at home—

a career in the navy offered a way up. Naval officers (and army officers) helped make up the central level of the middle class. A young man intent on becoming an officer in the Royal Navy first secured a berth as a midshipman in his teens. This could be accomplished through a system of "interest," or family connections, with the captain of a naval vessel. After six years as a midshipman, he was eligible to take an examination for the rank of lieutenant. The next higher rank was captain. Since the Victorian age saw few naval conflicts, there were not many openings for new captains. An ambitious lieutenant might wait decades to advance. Yet once he attained the rank of captain, the seniority system took over. A captain advanced as rear admirals, vice admirals, and full admirals retired or died.

The army operated on a different basis. Up until 1871 a young man had to purchase a commission in a particular regiment to enter the service as an officer. Only well-to-do families could afford a commission. Easily the most prestigious army regiments—and the most expensive to enter—were the Household Foot Guards and Household Cavalry. Among their duties was guarding the royal family. Less prestigious cavalry units included the dragoons, lancers, and hussars. The dragoons were mounted troops who sometimes fought on foot; the lancers carried military spears called lances into battle; and the hussars were modeled after Hungarian light cavalry troops and wore a flamboyant uniform. Ranked at the bottom of the military hierarchy were the infantry, or common foot soldiers. These troops included grenadiers, taller soldiers equipped with grenades. Soldiers were paid working-class salaries and were not considered middle-class, although officers were. As Pool relates, military life was far from glamorous:

Officers in the dragoons pose for a portrait in 1863. Positions in the dragoons and other cavalry units offered very little prestige, glamour, and pay.

The army as a whole was treated miserably by the English for most of the 1800s. They were quartered in the Tower of London and in local ale houses until [Prime Minister William] Pitt got them barracks to live in. . . . They were fed only two meals a day (beef—and only three-quarters of a pound of it at that—plus bread) with the consequence that they were often sick and hungry, and drank heavily to compensate for it.[25]

An officer might be transferred with his regiment to faraway locations such as India, Afghanistan, or the West Indies for years at a time. In such exotic surroundings, troops were exposed to malaria and other tropical diseases which were often fatal. Treatment at home was not much better. Over much of Victoria's reign, military officers and their men were not awarded pensions, and old age often brought poverty and illness.

On the Beat

After a career in Her Majesty's navy or army, some sailors or soldiers found a new career protecting city streets and rural villages. In London, they were known as the officers of the Metropolitan Police. Created in 1829 by Sir Robert Peel, constables of the Metro Police were full-time, salaried officers. It was from their creator that two of their nicknames came: "bobbies" or "peelers." Their mission was to thwart street crime, prevent riots, discourage public drunkenness, break up fights, and reduce begging.

In each of London's seventeen police districts, eight constables walked their beats while a ninth remained in the station house on standby status. The nine constables were supervised by a sergeant. The sergeant—one of six-teen in each district—reported directly to the district superintendent, as did four inspectors.

If a man decided to become a constable, he had to meet certain requirements. He had to be at least 5 ft. 8 in. (1.73m) in height. Since most Britons were shorter than this, due to poor nutrition, the constable had a large physical presence. The candidate was required to undergo two weeks of training, and had to be able to handle strenuous physical duties. Once he was sworn in, the new constable who was unmarried lived and took his meals in the police barracks. Pay was low, but officers were permitted to earn extra money by managing crowds at theaters or knocking on doors early in the morning to waken working people.

Law enforcement took a leap forward with the creation of the Detective Department in 1842. It was headquartered at London's famous Scotland Yard. Eventually the agency was reorganized as the Criminal Investigation Department, with the additional assignment of guarding the Queen and her family. The training, prestige, education, and pay of the detectives were better than that of the constables. So was their discretion. "The Detective Force," wrote Charles Dickens in his magazine *Household Words* in 1850, "is so well chosen and trained, proceeds so systematically and quietly . . . and is always so calmly and steadily engaged in the service of the public, that the public really does not know enough of it."[26]

The Profession of Medicine

Unlike the military and police occupations, the professions involed work that was less physical and less dangerous. Doctors and lawyers were also required to be educated and licensed in their areas of expertise. But it had

Medical students observe as a surgery is performed in a London hospital in 1901. Doctors in Victorian England were required to have the proper training and to be licensed.

not always been this way, especially in the field of medicine. "[Before] 1858, the organizational structure of the medical profession was in near-chaos," scholar M. Jeanne Peterson writes. "Medical training varied from classical education and the study of Greek and Latin medical texts on the one hand, to broom-and-apron apprenticeship in an apothecary's shop on the other."[27] Finally, in 1858 reformers persuaded Parliament to approve a new medical act. The act outlawed training by apprenticeship and established a program of lectures designed to provide proper instruction to medical students. Applicants were required to

The attitude of many upper-middle-class Victorians regarding females and work was clear. "A lady," historian Lee Holcomb quotes one woman as saying in *Victorian Ladies at Work: Middle-Class Working Women in England and Wales, 1850–1914*, "must be a mere lady and nothing else. She must not work for profit or engage in any occupation that money can command." Yet for many women of the middle-class, survival meant working for a living.

Until the mid-1800s, suitable occupations for middle-class women were rare. After 1850, this began to change. Commercial and industrial enterprises expanded as never before. As the size of business offices grew, so did the amount of clerical work required to keep them running. In businesses such as insurance, banking, advertising, and publishing, the swelling ranks of clerical workers came to make up a significant part of the workforce. To help fill the growing need, employers began hiring more women. As a rule, female employees were paid only between one-half and three-fifths of a man's salary for the same or similar work. Men still dominated the clerical field in number, but Victorian women showed extraordinary gains. An 1861 survey found more than 91,000 men working as clerks in England and Wales. Women accounted for fewer than 300. Twenty years later, the number of male clerks had swelled to nearly 230,000, while their female coworkers had increased to 6,420.

take examinations designed to weed out the unqualified. Passing the exams depended on ability alone, not wealth or position.

Medical practitioners fell into one of three distinct divisions in the early–to-mid-nineteenth century: physicians, surgeons, or apothecaries. Pool explains the difference:

> Physicians had the most prestige in 1800. . . . They were called physicians because they only administered drugs, or "physic." They did not deal with external injuries or perform surgery or set bones or do physical exams, other than of the patient's pulse and urine. They took detailed case histories and then wrote out a prescription to be filled by an apothecary. . . .
>
> Next below the physicians in the medical hierarchy were the surgeons. They were the men who cut people open, dealt with fractures, skin diseases, V.D. [venereal diseases, transmitted by sexual contact], eye problems—anything, in short, for which a physician could not simply give a prescription. . . .
>
> The apothecary was the lowest man on the medical totem pole. He was originally only supposed to make up prescriptions for physicians, but in many areas there were no physicians, so the apothecary began giving advice, too.[28]

Whether they wrote prescriptions or merely filled them, Victorian medical workers seldom became wealthy. Their salaries usually depended on the financial standing of the institutions that employed them. Not every physician earned a hefty salary. Doctors who treated patients in hospitals that served the poor might struggle to earn a living. One such hospital was busy St. Bartholomew's in London. Dr. Norman Moore wrote this account in 1869 of a typical workday in the outpatients' section of the hospital:

> I sit in a little room and hold a pen [and] a little board. . . . Outside is a horde of patients. On Tuesday there were 270. I beckon to one and he comes. . . . I ask his name and write it, the date and my own name on a bit of paper on my small board. I then ask him what is the matter and how long he has been ill, how much he drinks a day, and if he had been in the hospital before, and make my own observations on his symptoms.
>
> I then diagnose his disease: if it seems bad, or a chronic [recurring] case, I give him an outpatient's letter and send him over to the Assistant Physician. If the case seems slight . . . I write a prescription for the patient and tell him when to call again. He takes my prescription over to the dispensary [pharmacy] and receives the medicine at once. If I cannot make out the case I consult Mr. Jukes, a House Physician.[29]

In and out of Court

The medical field was not the only profession with gradually improving standards. The legal profession had its own divisions and methods of qualifying those interested in working in law. English lawyers were divided

Lawyers argue a case before the judge during a deer poaching case in 1888. Lawyers who argued at court occupied a higher social rank than those who did not.

into two categories. The first group comprised all those who actually argued cases in court: barristers, serjeants, and advocates. Each of these legal professionals pleaded in different segments of the English court system, such as the Chancery, King's Bench, and Admiralty Court. The second group was made up of solicitors, who did not argue in court. Instead they prepared cases to be presented by the lawyers who did.

At the top of the lawyer ladder was the barrister. He was often wellborn, commanded the stiffest fees, and enjoyed the highest social standing. A barrister's wife, for example, could be presented to the queen; a solicitor's wife could not. Barristers had their own Inns of Court in London, known as the Inner Temple, the Middle Temple, Lincoln's Inn, and Gray's Inn. Here in this combination of law school, offices, and apartments, lawyers and law students alike studied, worked, and lived.

Senior barristers called benchers took meals with prospective barristers "in Hall," where an unusual qualifying process took place. Pool describes the tradition:

> Until the latter part of the century, no exams were required of those who wished to become barristers. The sole requirement was to "eat your terms," that is, to show up for dinner a certain number of times for at least three years so the older lawyers could meet you informally and see if they approved of you. If . . . they found your work and character satisfactory, you were "called to the bar." . . . [This was] a small barrier, presumably in the Hall, that separated the area where the senior lawyers, or benchers, sat from where those who had not yet been called were. You were thereafter entitled to appear before the courts as a barrister. [30]

The Gentleman Farmer

On the social ladder of country life, the landowner occupied the top rung. He might be an aristocrat who inherited his land, or a member of the gentry—men of wealth who had purchased their land. The bottom rung was held by the lower class laborers. In the middle was the farmer who rented parcels of land from the wealthy landowner and hired laborers to work them.

Somewhere in the mid- to upper-middle classes was the another figure: the self-described "gentlemen farmer." These smaller landowners, once called yeomen, owned land they farmed themselves. On smaller farms of 100 acres or less, the gentleman farmer and his own family maintained the property. On the larger farms of 500 acres or more, he employed laborers to help him. The gentleman farmer might be only comfortably off or some of them were even wealthy. In *Victorian England*, historian W.J. Reader tells of one such farmer named William Till, who kept a diary:

On ordinary days he would get up and, as he put it, "set the men to rights" [gave them their instructions for the day's work]. Then he might spend the day in work about the farm—or he might not. He shot [hunted], he fished, he dug out badgers, he sang with the village glee club [chorus], and he visited his friends and relations. Of one typical evening he records "had tea & sundry games of wist [whist] . . . lost [a little money], spent a very enjoyable evening. Arrived home after a pleasant ride [at] 3:15 A.M."

Even in the legal profession, social status —or the appearance of it—was never forgotten. A prospective client could not hire a barrister or serjeant directly. Instead he engaged a solicitor or attorney to obtain those services. When the time came to pay legal fees, the client paid the solicitor to pay the barrister. "This peculiar setup enabled barristers and serjeants to pretend they were not 'in trade,' since it removed from them the necessity of taking money directly in payment for their services," Pool explains.[31]

Middle-Class Progress

For all the struggle of the middle class to gain respectability, its accomplishments were many. Most of the progress in industry, science and invention, transportation, exploration, and social reform made during Victoria's reign was made by the middle class. Fueling this astonishing string of advancements was a level of energy, confidence, and creativity rarely seen in England's history. "They caused the railways and the bridges, the tarred roads and the canals to be constructed," Evans and Evans write. "They traced the source of the Nile [River] and unearthed the stones of Ninevah [an ancient city in western Asia]. They built the factories and the stores, the town halls and the art galleries."[32] For the English men and women who belonged to the middle class, it was a time of new possibilities. It was their very success that posed a threat to the security and prestige of England's upper classes.

CHAPTER 3
"Unfit for People:" The Lower Classes at Home

If making a living was a daily battle for the lower classes, making a home was not much easier. Running a household, if only a poor one, cost money. The expense of food, clothing, and washing was often beyond the reach of a poor family. The most common necessities were often in short supply, or simply not attainable. While some members of the working classes fared somewhat better, the obstacles for poorer Victorian families remained daunting. City-fed pollution, unsafe housing, little or no sanitation, poor-quality food, and long working hours made maintaining a home a difficult and exhausting business.

Back to Back, Side to Side

The poorest urban Victorians lived in the oldest sections of a city, often little more than grimy slums. In the previous century, houses for middle-class workers had generally been designed in a back-to-back style, with each tenant sharing the rear and side walls with his or her neighbors. As the decades passed, these buildings became deserted, left behind by wealthier people moving out of the cities into the suburbs. Into these abandoned structures moved a different level of tenant—the lower class. Reader points out,

> Where one family had lived in comfort— even affluence—under George VI [William IV's predecessor], as many families as the place had rooms might live under the middle-aged or elderly Victoria. Late in the 20th century it is [still] possible to see, in many large English towns, successive belts of shabby property . . . which, like the growth rings of a tree, mark the outward expansion of the town. [33]

Space was the greatest problem. There were simply not enough buildings in which to house the swelling tide of the poor. When ground-floor rooms were not to be had, those seeking shelter crowded into garrets (attic rooms) and cellars. Where crowding was the worst, a family considered itself fortunate to have even a single room in which to live. In the most severe cases, six or eight people of both genders might share one room. A few soiled blankets served as a bed. Infants and toddlers had neither cradle nor crib to sleep in. With living space at a premium, younger children shared a bed with their older siblings. If they were lucky, the residents might have a fire grate on which to cook food. Illumination was provided by a few tallow candles which gave off a dim, flickering light. A few might even have oil lamps. (Gaslight would not be widely used indoors until the 1880s.)

Overcrowding raised moral issues well. In the 1850s, a Unitarian missionary named Edward Hall was appalled by the workingclass cottages he observed in the town of Leeds:

> They are built back to back, with no possibility of good ventilation, and contain a cellar for coals and food . . . a room from

9 to 14 feet by from 12 to 14 feet, to do all the cooking, washing, and the necessary work of a family, and another of the same size for all to sleep in. Think for a moment what must be the inconvenience, the danger both in a moral and physical sense, when parents and children, young men and women, married and single, are crowded together in this way, with three beds in a room, and barely a couple of yards in the middle for the whole family to undress and dress in.[34]

The problems of poorly constructed housing for the lower working class did not go unnoticed by government officials. In 1885 the Royal Commission on the Housing of the Working Classes investigated English living conditions and was highly critical of substandard construction practices. "'Jerry building' [shoddy construction] is too well known," the commission report read. "The houses are often built of the commonest materials, and with the worst workmanship, and are altogether unfit for people to live in."[35] Despite the promise of reforms, change in the housing industry was slow in coming. And before change did arrive, the unhealthy conditions common to poor housing was to exact a heavy toll in human health and life.

Hazardous to Their Health

To make the most of small plots of land, builders put up houses with little or no space in between. In these structures it was difficult for fresh air to circulate. Smoke and soot

Children sit and women gossip in the courtyard of a Victorian slum building, while laundry dries overhead and chickens roam free.

from the cooking fires and chimneys hung in the air, coating everything. Sanitation was virtually nonexistent. In the early years of the era, there was no running water, no water closets (toilets), and no sewer systems. Human waste was collected in buckets or "slop jars" and dumped into overflowing cesspools. Since street vehicles were drawn by horses, animal droppings littered the streets. Household refuse was merely tossed out windows and doors, where it collected in the gutters. Overcrowding, fetid air, poor circulation, and lack of drainage created breeding grounds for diseases such as cholera, typhoid, and typhus.

Unclean living conditions invited more unwelcome guests into the home. Rats, lice, fleas, and other vermin brought misery to members of poor families. The least harm they caused was irritation and discomfort. Social investigator Charles Booth visited houses on Shelton Street in London's St. Giles area and made this observation:

Fifteen rooms out of twenty were filthy to the last degree. . . . Not a room would be

Diseases of the Slums

Of the many diseases that sickened and killed lower-class Victorians, cholera was one of the worst. Fatal to half of its victims, cholera was caused by the presence of human waste in drinking water. It was virtually unknown in England until 1831, when it arrived from India. In its first seven months, the disease killed twenty-two thousand Englishmen. During Victoria's reign, outbreaks of cholera wiped out nearly one hundred thousand. Not only was cholera deadly, but it spread and killed with terrible speed. Historian Christopher Hibbert describes the progression of the disease in *The English: A Social History, 1066–1945*:

"The most frightening aspect of the disease was the suddenness with which its victims perished. An attack of violent diarrhea and vomiting was followed by agonizing cramps in the limbs and abdomen, thirst and fever. After three to twelve hours, the symptoms advanced with rapidity, the skin became dry and a dusky blue or purple in color, the eyes sank in their sockets, the features were pinched, the pulse at the wrist imperceptible, the voice reduced to a hoarse whisper. Death often took place within a day, sometimes in a few hours."

A similar disease was an inflammation of the intestines also caused by contaminated food or water, called typhoid. Another was typhus, an infection of the blood spread from person to person by body lice or fleas. Typhus was as common as it was deadly. Diphtheria, scarlet fever, bronchitis, and pneumonia also brought their share of human misery to the slums of England. Periodic epidemics of all these illnesses killed perhaps two hundred thousand men, women, and children throughout the nineteenth century.

Other nonfatal diseases threatened Britons' health. Rickets twisted the limbs and stunted the growth of working-class children. It was caused by a lack of both sunlight and vitamin D in the diet. Catarrh developed in the presence of polluted and smoky air, and inflamed the nose, sinuses, and throat, making breathing difficult. Government reforms demanding new health codes and updated sewer systems would not arrive until the 1860s and 1870s.

free from vermin, and in many life at night was unbearable. Several occupants have said that in hot weather they don't go to bed, but sit in their clothes in the least infected part of the room. What good is it, they said, to go to bed when you can't get a wink of sleep for bugs and fleas?[36]

Adding to sanitation problems in Victorian-era cities was the shortage of fresh water for drinking and cooking. By the early 1800s, water mains had been installed to transport clean water under the newer and more prominent streets of many cities. Since housing for the poor was located back among the maze of older lanes and alleys, this source of water was not readily available. Entire lower-class neighborhoods might be served by a single stand-pipe—a water pump extending above the pavement—that might dispense water to residents for less than an hour each day. For some people, this proved to be very inconvenient. Reader recounts the following conversation between a government worker and a slum resident in the city of Bath in 1840:

> *Resident:* [Water] is as valuable as strong beer. We can't use it for cooking, or anything of that sort, but only for drinking and tea.
>
> *Interviewer:* Then where do you get water for cooking and washing?

FUN.—AUGUST 18, 1866.

DEATH'S DISPENSARY.
OPEN TO THE POOR, GRATIS, BY PERMISSION OF THE PARISH.

This 1863 cartoon uses the figure of Death pumping a well to comment on the quality of London's water supply.

> *Resident:* Why, from the river. But it is muddy, and often stinks bad, because all the filth is carried there.
>
> *Interviewer:* Do you prefer to cook your victuals [food] in water which is muddy and stinks to walking a quarter of a mile to fetch it from the pump?

"Unfit for People:" The Lower Classes at Home

Resident: We can't help ourselves, you know. We couldn't go all that way for it. [37]

It would be another three or four decades before improved water systems were extended to the poorer sections of the nation's cities. In some locations, improved systems never came at all. By then, thousands more lower-class citizens had died from diseases carried by fouled water, including cholera and typhoid.

Home Versus Work

For the lower classes, leisure time spent with family was rare. With parents laboring twelve to fourteen hours per day, and their older children working about the same hours, opportunities for interaction were scarce. Younger girls stayed home to look after infants and smaller siblings, and to help their mothers. When the mother was working, a girl might spend between twenty and thirty hours per week on housework, errands, and tending the children.

Parents were often obliged to take their smaller children to work with them. In the workplace, conditions were often no better for the children than those at home. Novelist and social critic Charles Dickens made these observations while visiting a weaver's shop in Spitalfields in 1851:

> The room is unwholesome, close and dirty. . . . The looms claim all the superior space and have it. Like grim enchanters who provide the family with their scant food, they must be propitiated [appeased] with the best accommodation. They [the looms] bestride the room, and pitilessly squeeze the children—this heavy, watery-headed baby carried in the arms of its staggering little

brother, for example—into corners. The children sleep at night between the legs of the monsters, who deafen their first cries with their whirr and rattle. [38]

When parents were unable to care for small children either at home or at work, the older children were forced to take up the slack, even if they too worked. In 1849 Mayhew noted the comments of one child who combined work with child care:

> I'm twelve years old, please, sir, and my name is Margaret R——, and I sweep a crossing in New Oxford Street. . . . Mother's been dead these two years, sir, and father's a working cutler, sir . . . and so I'm obligated to help him, doing what I can, sir. Since Mother's been dead, I've had to mind my little brother and sister, so that I haven't been to school; but when I goes a crossing sweeping I takes them along with me, and they sits on the steps close by, sir. If it's wet I has to stop at home and take care of them, for father depends upon me for looking after them. Sister's three-and-a-half year old, and brother's five year, so he's just beginning to help me, sir. . . .
>
> I generally takes about sixpence, or sevenpence, or eightpence on the crossing, from about nine o'clock in the morning till four in the evening, when I come home. I don't stop out at nights because father won't let me, and [I've] got to be home to see to baby. [39]

Time and Money

The hours spent at home by working members of a lower-class household were few. This point is underscored by an 1841 account

The dreaded workhouse was Victorian England's "second home" for lower-class Britons fallen on hard times. Workhouses were not designed to provide relief for people who refused to work, but for those who, temporarily or otherwise, were unable to support themselves.

Ordinarily, a family applied to enter the workhouse when the chief bread-winner was sick or injured, and all other resources had been exhausted. When (and if) the family was again able to support itself, they were allowed to leave. Yet, as George Edwards learned in 1855, entry was not always voluntary. His account is related by Christabel Orwin and Edith Whetham in *History of British Agriculture, 1846–1914*.

"On my father's return home from work one night he was stopped by a policeman, who searched his bag and took from it five turnips, which he was taking to make his children an evening meal. . . . His wife and children were waiting for him to come home, but he was not allowed to do so. He was arrested, taken before the magistrate the next day, and committed to 14 days'

hard labor for the crime of attempting to feed his children!"

Once inside, inmates were clothed in coarse uniforms and grouped by age and gender. Children were separated from parents, husbands from wives, and placed in separate wards. The sick and the mentally ill were housed in the same building as orphans and unwed mothers. Outside visitors were discouraged; receiving gifts was forbidden. For weeks or even months on end, the residents were forced to spend long hours performing such tasks as cooking, cleaning, or sewing. Some inmates nursed other inmates, or helped bury the dead. Others worked at breaking stones for gravel, or picking oakum [tarred strands of fiber used in shipbuilding] from ropes, a task which tortured the fingers and nails. The wards where the inmates slept were often dirty and the food barely edible. One dish was "skilly," a foul concoction of cornmeal boiled in water.

The stated aim of the workhouse was to make its conditions so dreadful that people would do anything to avoid going there. Most people did.

of a young female factory worker in Manchester. It first appeared in labor advocate William Dodd's book *The Factory System Illustrated*. The young woman's day begins at 4:30 A.M., when the town's night watchman raps on the window to waken the workers in the household. Her mother

rouses the unwilling girl to another day of toil. At length you hear her on the floor; the clock is striking five . . . having slipped on her clothes, and (if she thinks there is time) washed herself, she takes a drink of

cold coffee, which has been left standing in the fireplace, a mouthful of bread (if she can eat it), and having packed up her breakfast in her handkerchief, hastens to the factory. . . .

Every day . . . she came in at half-past twelve [during her dinner hour] . . . the first thing she did was to wash herself, then get her dinner (which she was seldom able to eat), and pack up her drinking for the afternoon. This done, it was time to be on her way to work again, where she remains, without one minute's relaxation, till seven o'clock; she then comes home, and throws herself into a chair exhausted. [40]

Even when people were not exhausted from a long workday, the evening had little to offer in the way of relaxation and recreation. There were no sofas to recline upon, no televisions to watch, or computer games to play. The absence of electricity and the expense of candles limited activities such as sewing or indoor games. Poor lighting as well as illiteracy all but eliminated reading as a leisure pastime.

The problems facing home life caused by a shortage of free time were compounded by a shortage of money. A city family of five described as "very poor" might have a weekly income of 15 shillings, or three-quarters of one pound. Nine shillings of this amount would be spent on food. Rent, lighting, and heating would consume more than five shillings more. The family might spend the tiny remainder— a few pence—on clothing or some other necessity. Thus the entire earnings for the week would be used up. Throughout the week, one of the few pleasures a working family could look forward to was food.

Bless This Bread (and Sometimes Meat)

Dinner for lower-class Victorians was simple at best. Without refrigeration, food items in the house were limited to what could be easily stored for a day or two without spoiling. As a result, poor people shopped for food often and bought small amounts. They did most of their purchasing from bakers and street sellers who peddled bread, meat pies, roasted potatoes, pea soup (also known as "pease porridge"), smoked herring, and coffee.

Bread was the chief feature of the working-class diet. "It's not all poor people [who] can get meat; but they must get bread," [41] declared an anonymous observer of the working classes. Working women had little time to prepare meals and often turned to bread and potatoes for weekday dinners. Bread required no further preparation, and potatoes were easily boiled in a pot over the fire. When the family budget allowed, butter, sugar, cheese, fish, and tea supplemented the weekly menu. (Tea was drinkable because the water was boiled beforehand.) To spice up their usually drab meals, lower-class families sometimes added meat drippings or small amounts of bacon to food. On those rare occasions when meat was available for a Sunday or holiday meal, poorer families dispensed with cooking. Instead they carried their beef or pork dishes to the local baker for roasting. Any available meat or other extras were given to the family breadwinners first—sometimes only the father and sons—since it was thought they needed the additional energy. Overall, lower-class diets offered little in the way of protein or fat.

In time, the nutritional value of working-class diets improved. Advances in refrigeration technology made it possible for meat and fish to be kept chilled for transporation from seaports to inland locations. An expanded railway system and faster locomotives reduced travel time for food and other goods. These improvements lowered prices and enabled many working families to introduce eggs, milk, margarine, jam, and other perishables into their diets for the first time.

Across the Countryside

Squalid living conditions, unfortunately, were not restricted to the cities. Farm laborers in

The Shirts on Their Backs

For poorer Victorians, there was no such thing as fashion. People struggling for their next meal gave little thought to the fullness of a lady's skirts or the cut of a gentleman's coat. As much as possible, clothes were made at home; previously worn garments could be purchased cheaply from street vendors or in secondhand shops.

Lower-class females wore full-skirted dresses made of inexpensive cotton, often with an apron. Beneath the skirts, linen petticoats covered the lower part of the body. Women seldom went outdoors without covering their heads with a cloth cap, a bonnet, or a scarf. In cooler weather, a shawl helped ward off the chill.

Men wore long trousers of thick cotton fabric, often a coarse material called fustian. Their shirts were made of linsey-woolsey, an inexpensive blend of linen and wool. Over their shirts, they sported a plain waistcoat and some sort of coat. Men completed their outfits with a billed cap or soft felt hat. In some cases, a discarded top hat added a touch of "elegance."

Children dressed much like their parents, except in miniature. Toddlers, both girls and boys, wore dresses that reached to their ankles. A boy might receive his first pair of trousers around the age of four. A young girl's skirts usually stopped between the knee and ankle. Sometime during her teens, she would begin wearing full-length skirts and dresses to underscore her passage to womanhood. Most clothing for poor children was either hand-me-downs from siblings or secondhand adult garments cut down to size. For all ages, getting shoes and boots was a challenge because they were expensive new and hard to find used.

Wash day for the poor was an irregular event. While those living in the country could wash their clothes in rivers and streams, poor urban people had no such convenience. City dwellers were forced to use the community standpipe for the necessary water. Since they competed with hundreds of people for it, getting enough water for laundry was difficult.

---

the country endured their share of unhealthy, even dangerous, conditions. Crowding in rural housing was less severe than in cities, but farmworkers often lived in cottages containing no more than one or two rooms, the second above the first. Often poorly built and badly ventilated, the structures were dark, drafty, and damp. "You will find between the Mendips and the fashionable watering-place known as Weston-super-Mare," reported one witness to the 1885 Royal Commission, "that you can hardly call the dwellings cottages, for some of them are only lean-to roofs up against the wall."[42] In the better buildings, a sizable fireplace provided adequate warmth for heating and flames for cooking. For privacy for bathing or dressing, a rope might be strung across the interior and draped with a blanket to form a curtain. The floor was made of tightly packed earth or paving stones. A rough table, a couple of benches or crude chairs, and a cooking pot or two made up the typical house's meager furnishings.

The general condition of a farming village depended on who owned it. In many cases, one well-to-do resident owned most or all of the land in the area. Local farmers not only worked his land, often on tracts rented by the farmer, but lived in housing he supplied. If the landlord was conscientious, he

A family of farmworkers sitting on the ground outside their home shares a meal. Living conditions in the Victorian countryside were typically squalid.

kept his dwellings decently maintained for the good of his workers. In villages where farmland and homesteads were in the hands of many landlords, the quality of housing generally suffered. The cottages were often allowed to weather and decay, and residents had little recourse for improvements.

Like their urban counterparts, rural lower-class Britons had to depend on wealthier Britons for their housing, as well as their employment. This left them at the mercy of property owners who were not always conscientious in the upkeep of their holdings. This problem was seldom experienced by the rural poor's "betters." For the middle and upper classes, home was a symbol of their success or birth, not a squalid reminder of their lack of either.

"The Crystal of Society:" Home for the Middle and Upper Classes

"The Home is the crystal of society," wrote the Victorian observer Samuel Smiles in 1859, "the very nucleus of national character."[43] If any level of British society valued the home, it was the middle class. Unlike the aristocrats, they worked for their housing and furnishings. Unlike the lower classes, they worked fewer hours at higher pay and thus had more time to enjoy their homes.

It was in the Victorian era that the middle-class idea of family came into its own. For inspiration, Britons needed only to look to their monarch. Queen Victoria, her husband, Prince Albert, and their children were the first closely-knit royal family the English had seen in many years. The obvious affection the regal parents lavished on their nine offspring was noted with the greatest interest by their subjects. Intentionally or not, Victoria, Albert, and their children served as models for what family life at its best could be. Yet for all of its advantages, middle- and upper-class home life did have its negative side. Unlike the royal family, well-to-do parents did not always enjoy a close, affectionate relationship with their children.

The royal family, pictured here with Victoria and Albert at the center, was celebrated as the paragon of family life in Victorian England.

A Roof over Their Heads

The most obvious sign of a family's status was the home. Few middle-class Britons actually owned homes. Instead they leased their houses from rich landlords for terms of three, five, or seven years. Limited available land meant that urban houses were built narrow and tall. Erected in rows with no structures behind, lower-middle-class homes rose as high as four stories and contained seven or eight rooms.

The lowest floor of each house was situated half below street level and half above. Called the area, this story provided a delivery and service entrance, and the main work space for the servants. The pantry, kitchen, and scullery (where laundry and other tasks requiring water were handled) were located here. On the same floor were the entrance hall, dining room (placed conveniently near the kitchen), and a room known variously as the study, library, or office. This space was allotted to the man of the house for his personal use. If he ran his own professional business, such as a medical or law practice, he might see his clients in this room. The woman of the house received no such space.

The second floor—known by the English as the first floor—housed the rooms designed for family recreation and entertaining. The largest was the drawing room, where the host

A Briton's home was the most obvious sign of his or her social status. Houses in the city were built narrow and tall to conserve land.

and hostess received guests for conversation and light refreshments. Only when no such company was present could the children of the household entertain themselves there.

The third floor included bedrooms for the family. This area provided a nursery for the younger children for daytime and nighttime use, with sleeping space for their nursemaid. Older children shared quarters with siblings of the same gender until the age of eight or nine. The adults' bedroom might offer separate dressing rooms for the husband and wife to afford more privacy when they wished.

The fourth floor contained living space for the servants as well as a storage area. A set of back stairs ran from this floor to the basement. It allowed servants to tote food or other items to different levels of the house out of view of family or guests.

They Called It "Home"

The popular arrangement for houses of the upper middle class was three or four structures in single rows that faced all four sides of a square. A single residence for the very richest might take up one entire side. Inside the square was a pleasant area with grass, shrubs, and perhaps a few trees. The houses themselves were much like those of the lower middle class, only larger and more opulent. The typical upper-middle-class home was crowded with potted palms and other living plants, heavily patterned wallpaper, bird cages with parrots or cockatiels, painted fire screens, clusters of family pictures, paintings, and various bric-a-brac. The entrance hall might feature an ornate front door, an Oriental rug on a stone floor, and an umbrella stand, often in the shape of some exotic creature.

In the larger houses, a bright, well-lit morning room supplied space for women's activities. In smaller homes, the drawing room served that function. Couches, plush chairs, and perhaps a piano furnished the area. In the center stood a sizable circular table covered by a cloth. Coffee or tea were served from this table, or it could be used for sewing and embroidery, looking at large books or albums, or playing cards and other games. Ladies wrote letters and made out menus for social gatherings in this room.

The homes of the aristocracy were handed down from father to firstborn son, and had been for perhaps centuries. Often they resembled castles as much as houses, and might include a billiard room, a smoking room, and other special areas. Every room of size featured a fireplace. Only the wealthiest homeowners, however, kept fires going regularly in their bedrooms—a luxury, even by upper-class standards.

Not to be outdone by the aristocracy, untitled men of money hurried to imitate them. They paid the best available architects and builders to create impressive new residences in the country. Like the homes of the highborn, the mansions of the recently rich occupied expansive grounds dotted with gardens, greenhouses, outbuildings, and stables. Stables were a special symbol of affluence and independence. In country or city, only the wealthy could afford to purchase and maintain horses and carriages.

Middle-Class Households

Inside the home, Victorians observed a strict ranking of roles. In the middle-class household, the father was the undisputed master. He was not merely the chief breadwinner in the family, he was the only breadwinner. His wife did not have an income of her own. Her husband, therefore, exercised complete economic and legal control over her, their children, and their servants. He was also responsible for all household debts. To pay for it all, a father in business or a profession worked long hours away from home. He took lunch at his club—a private establishment where middle-class men spent their free time—or a restaurant, and did not return home before seven o'clock in the evening.

His wife had few legal rights. "On her marriage," historian Charles Petrie explains, "a girl usually passed from dependence upon parents to submission to a husband." She did not work at a job or profession. Unless she came from a family rich enough to provide a private source of funds, she had no financial resources. Any property or goods she may have owned before marrying automatically became her husband's. "The conception of marriage as a partnership," Petrie adds, "was quite unknown."[44]

In effect, Victorian society trained the middle- and upper-class female to be dependent upon marriage. Her schooling—music, art, literature, and how to carry and conduct herself—was aimed at making her attractive to an eligible man, and little else. "The real tragedy was that although the Victorian girl was skilled in the art of acquiring a husband, she was . . . given no training of any sort in

The Rich and the Richer

In all of England, no more than three thousand or four thousand families could have been called extremely rich. Of the untitled wealthy, the landed gentry were by far the richest; they reaped their riches from renting sections of their land to others to farm. In effect, they did not work for a living; neither did upper-class Victorians who did not own land, but received an income earned on investments made with inherited money. Yet in class-conscious Victorian England, income was one thing and position in society another. Money did not dictate a person's rung on the social ladder. An impassible barrier lay between aristocrat and commoner, one that could not be crossed by riches alone. That barrier—one that no Briton was allowed to forget—was blood. Whether duke or baron, viscount or earl, aristocrats received their titles and riches through a simple biological process —birth. Around the time Victoria became queen, there were some 560 titled families in England, and they wielded awesome power. "They controlled Great Britain herself, to an extent that would be inconceivable in any civilized nation today," writes historian William Manchester in the introduction to Winston Churchill's autobiography *My Early Life: 1874–1904*. "One percent of the country's population—some 33,000 people — owned two-thirds of its wealth, and that wealth . . . was breathtaking." The 250 richest aristocrats enjoyed an annual income of as much as 30,000 pounds, or around 1,750,000 pounds in today's British currency.

The upper middle class pulled in a handsome income as well, but their top earnings fell far below the incomes of the aristocrats. The richest merchants, bankers, and manufacturers earned as much as ten thousand pounds a year, one-third as much as the wealthiest aristocrats, yet one hundred times the yearly income of a carpenter or senior dressmaker. Further down the scale, farm laborers and typists did well to clear thirty pounds in a year. To these modest-living Britons, the lifestyles of the aristocracy must have seemed the stuff of fairy tales.

her practical duties as a wife," Petrie continues. "She was quite untrained in household management."[45] And yet much was expected of her. In *The Book of Household Management*, a famous 1861 advice manual, Mrs. Isabella Beeton paints a lofty portrait:

> As with the Commander of an Army, so it is with the mistress of a house. . . . Of all those acquirements which more particularly belong to the feminine character, there are none which take on a higher rank than such as enter into a knowledge of household duties; for on these are perpetually dependent the happiness, comfort and well-being of a family.[46]

Both middle- and upper-class families employed servants. Middle-class households might have from two to four servants, while upper-class homes might require a dozen or more. Because the servants cared for her children, prepared meals, and cleaned house, there might be little for the mistress of the house to do. Accordingly, upper-class wives filled their days with rounds of social calls on friends, and with costly shopping trips. Many women found time to become involved in charity work. Evenings found them either giving extravagant dinners at home or attending them elsewhere with their husbands. Middle-class mothers with only two or three servants could seldom afford such activities.

The Children

"My mother made [a] brilliant impression upon my childhood's eye," recalled British statesman and World War II leader Winston

The future Queen Victoria is pictured with her nurse. Many upper-class parents left the rearing of their children to nannies and other servants.

Churchill. "She shone for me like the Evening Star. I loved her dearly—but at a distance. My nurse was my confidante. Mrs. Everest it was who looked after me and tended all my wants. It was to her I poured out my many troubles."[47]

Many children of upper-middle-class and elite families were raised under similar conditions. Victorian parents loved their children,

Coin of the Realm

The names for British coins and currency, pounds, shillings, and pence, have often been vague, if not downright confusing, for Americans to understand. Passing decades and rising inflation have only compounded the confusion. But in her book *Daily Life in a Victorian House*, teacher and author Laura Wilson offers this breakdown of British money during the Victorian era:

"Before Britain had decimal currency, the money was known as 'l, s, and d.' These letters stand for the Latin words *librae, solidi,* and *denarii*, meaning pounds, shillings, and pence. There were 12d to one shilling (now 5 pence or about 8 cents U.S. currency) and 20 shillings—or 240d to £1. The smallest coin was a 'farthing' which was worth a quarter of one penny. The bank notes were much bigger in size than modern ones— 8 1/8" by 5 1/4". Their values were £5, £10, £20, £100, £200, £300, £500, and £1000. During the 1870s and 1880s, £1 was worth £30 of today's money, so a £1,000 note was equivalent to £30,000 or $51,000 in U.S. dollars now [as of 1993]!"

---

but believed in a little distance. They were content to leave the everyday tasks of parenting to people they considered merely servants—nurses, nannies, and governesses. This attitude was evident even in the layout of the house; children and their caregivers were often given their own separate wing. This arrangement allowed more space for schoolrooms, nurseries, and sleeping areas. But there was another benefit. Hailing "the principle of Privacy," an 1864 pamphlet titled *The Gentleman's House* declared that "the main part of the house must be relieved from the more immediate occupation of the children."[48]

It is not surprising that many Victorian children, like the young Churchill, formed a special bond of affection with their nurse or nanny. "She reads them stories, looks after them when they are ill, and comforts them when they are unhappy," author Laura Wilson points out. "They tell her secrets that they would not dream of telling their parents."[49] The nurse's supervision was nearly constant.

A typical weekday began around eight o'clock with prayers before breakfast. Roused by their nurse, the children trooped down stairs to the family dining room. Joining them were the rest of the servants, and mother and father, who led the group in prayer. It was the last time the children would see their father that day. They were immediately hustled back up to the nursery while the cook finished preparing breakfast. Father and mother were served in the dining room, while the children's food was brought upstairs. When father left for his office, mother retired to the parlor to do the household accounts.

Once the children were dressed, the nurse or governess took them out to the nearby park for a walk. The children were allowed to play with the neighbor children while their nurse passed the time with other nurses and nannies. Back in the nursery, the children were given lessons by the governess until lunchtime. Like breakfast, this meal was also eaten in the nursery. Lunch was followed by a rest period and then more time to play inside. An hour or two later, the children stopped for afternoon tea. At around five o'clock, they changed into fresh clothes for an hour's visit with mother in the drawing room. Upstairs again, the nurse bathed them in water that had been warmed on the kitchen fire and hauled up to the nursery. By around 6:30 P.M., the children had said their prayers and were in bed. Their nurse slept either in the same room or the one adjacent.

At the Table

The foods eaten by middle- and upper-class Victorians were more abundant, more varied, and more nutritious than those of the lower class. The centerpiece of most meals was meat, often two or three different kinds—something a chimney sweep or flower seller could only dream of. Until refrigeration was invented later in the century, the upper classes also relied on the local food supply for fresh edibles. The cook or mistress of a household purchased food from tradespeople who called every day at the kitchen door. Taking advantage of this home delivery service, the larders of rich families could be stocked with fresh meats, milk, eggs, fruits, and vegetables on a daily basis.

Lower-middle-class diets were less varied. One businessman's wife outlined her family's typical weekday fare in 1901:

We had breakfast at a quarter to eight for my husband and the children to get off [to work and school] in time. He had a light lunch at an A.B.C. [an early restaurant franchise] in the City; they came home to dinner. We had tea at 6:30, cake and bread and jam, or sometimes macaroni cheese or anchovy toast or a pudding or cheese, and always a little dish for my husband because he didn't have midday dinner. If the children were hungry I'd make them a cup of tea and give them a bit of cake or bread-and-butter at half-past four. The maid had what we had. [50]

For the rich, breakfast was a large meal. In addition to bacon, other hot meats such as mutton and kidneys might be served. These were accompanied by eggs, English muffins or toast, marmalade, fruit, and a selection of cold meats. Coffee, tea, and cocoa were the preferred beverages. Milk was usually avoided. Until pasteurization was invented late in the century, milk carried germs that caused tuberculosis. Despite its generous portions, breakfast was a less formal meal than dinner, as the American writer Richard Henry Dana discovered during an 1875 stay at the Duke of Argyll's castle:

At breakfast the servants disappeared after putting the food on the sideboard and we helped ourselves or waited on one another. The ladies seemed to expect to wait on themselves, even the Princess [Louise, a daughter of Queen Victoria]. . . . It was all so very simple and informal. The talk at breakfast was cheery and pleasant. [51]

Luncheon at home usually featured cold meat or chops. If a hot meal was served, it was a light one. For children, who usually had an early bedtime, this was their main meal of the day. Later they ate a lighter snack before turning in. Lunch for adults might include bread and fruit, if available. Salads were practically unheard-of. The science of nutrition was still in the future; most people believed that eating raw vegetables was bad for the digestion.

Dinner at Eight

For the upper middle and higher classes, the final meal of the day was an extravagant affair. Company or no company, dinner never featured fewer than four courses. This included one or two kinds of meat, fish or fowl, vegetables,

For the upper classes, the evening meal was an extravagant affair with several courses. Dinner parties such as the one depicted here were especially festive.

fruit dishes, and a dessert. According to Mrs. Beeton's manual, a modest mid-week dinner might feature "1. Baked cod's head. 2. Cold mutton, roast hare [rabbit], gravy and red-currant jelly. 3. Macaroni."[52]

Adults usually drank wine with the meal. Afterward, they might treat themselves to a glass of a liqueur such as port, or to a cup of coffee. Even when no guests were present, family members came to the table dressed in their very best. At these family-only meals, one servant remained in the dining room to serve the different courses and tend to the diners' needs. When not serving, the servant

was positioned behind the mistress's chair and stood motionless until called upon.

But for sheer extravagance, nothing could match the formal dinner party. Invitations went out to the intended guests a week in advance. Every detail about the meal was carefully planned down to the last sauce and bottle of wine. The servants were rehearsed on etiquette and special duties; on the appointed evening, they would be expected to be efficient, silent, and next to invisible. At 7:30 or 8:00 P.M., the arriving guests were shown to the drawing room. Here the host paired up each gentleman with a lady, not his

Buying and maintaining a coach and horses was a luxury within the reach of few Victorians. Even fewer could also afford a second carriage or cart. It was a mark of status even children could understand, as Lord Ernest Hamilton recalled in writing of Chesterfield, his family's London home in the 1860s. Gillian Avery quotes Lord Hamilton in her book *Victorian People: In Life and Literature*.

"The coach-house hid a host of carriages of one kind or another, but . . . the most familiar object was my mother's barouche [an open carriage with facing seats, pulled by two horses], a noble equipage indeed, dark crimson paneled and hung high up on C springs. The spokes of the wheels were striped in crimson, black and yellow, and the heavy silver harness was relieved by huge rosettes of dark blue and white. (How we despised people whose harness was of common brass!) High up on the box [driver's seat] sat the great Busk, the head coachman, in breeches and silk stockings . . . and after a while an equally splendid footman climbed up to keep him company and off the black-brown horses would prance."

In the country, a well-to-do family might also own a governess cart to serve the children and their caregiver. Built low to the road, this high-sided cart was better balanced and less likely to tip. A nurse or governess could steer the vehicle to church or a social event with less risk to her precious charges.

Few Victorians could afford to buy and maintain their own coach and horses, so most used public transportation such as this coach.

wife, whom he would escort to the dining room. Married people were seated separately so that they might make conversation with the other guests more readily.

The favored style of service during the Victorian era was "dinner *a la russe*," so named because it was thought to have originated in Russia. Kristine Hughes describes the method:

> The table was laid out with both plate and glass and ornamented with flowers, with dessert being the only course to be laid directly upon the table. All of the food served during the preceding courses was first brought to the sideboard [a waist-high cupboard on slender legs]. From these bowls and platters, the butler took a portion of each dish and arranged each diner's meal upon a china plate, which was then placed in front of each guest. . . . It was this new method of serving dinner that brought about the necessity for menu cards. One of these cards was placed between every two diners, so that guests would know what foods were to be served.[53]

At the conclusion of dinner, servants cleared the table and brought out finger bowls, clean wine glasses, and dessert plates. Following dessert, the ladies rose and adjourned to the drawing room, where they were served coffee. The gentlemen remained at the dining-room table only long enough to enjoy a glass of port or brandy before joining the ladies once more for tea. By 10:30 or 11:00 P.M., the evening ended.

Pluses and Minuses

Home for the middle and upper classes meant safer, cleaner, and more spacious living conditions than those available to the lower classes. It could be, and was, enjoyed with little worry as to whether it would be there the next day. There was no overcrowding. Hunger was never a threat. Yet for all its comforts and prestige, middle- and upper-class family life had challenges of its own. The difficulties came not from poverty or poor living conditions but from the demands of society and the weight of tradition on the parents.

"Her Noblest Wealth:" Education in Victorian England

The Victorian era swept in a new view of the importance of learning. Once, education had been considered a luxury for the middle class, and a near impossibility for the poor. Whether a child was educated at all depended on such factors as income level, religion, social class, and gender. Yet as the decades passed, the notion that knowledge could empower even the lowest classes began to take hold. The poet William Wordsworth was one artist who urged the British government to take the lead in educating the masses:

> O for the coming of that glorious time
>
> When, prizing knowledge as her
>   noblest wealth
>
> And best protection, this imperial
>   Realm,
>
> While she exacts obedience, shall admit
>
> An obligation, on her part, to *teach*
>
> Them who were born to serve her
>   and obey. [54]

In time, Parliament responded by enacting laws to make education available to more Britons. And yet progress did not guarantee equality. Extensive learning, it was thought, was unnecessary for girls, and beliefs such as these were slow to change. Greater equality in public education was not achieved until well after Victoria's death.

Education Comes of Age

As the 1830s began, England's educational system was practically nonexistent. There was no centralized authority to set standards or supply funds for the few schools that did exist. Reform efforts stalled as politicians and church leaders wrangled over what to teach, whom to teach, and how to pay for it. But a growing social movement saw popular education as England's best hope for combating ignorance, poverty, and crime. By the start of Victoria's reign, the wheels of reform were already turning.

A variety of schools reached out to the poor and working class. The most successful of these were the elementary schools. Most were operated by charitable, voluntary, or religious societies. Between 1833 and 1858, Parliament increased the money it granted in aid to these schools by 300 percent. To protect its investment, the government created the Royal Commission on Popular Education in 1858 to evaluate elementary school performance. Special inspectors rated the students of each institution for attendance and academic achievement. The latter was measured by yearly examinations in reading, writing, and arithmetic, plus needlework for girls.

Over the next three decades, school reform became vitalized. In 1870 Parliament passed the Elementary Education Act, making these schools available to 5 million school-age

Victorian schoolboys pose for a class picture. By the end of the nineteenth century, primary education was provided to English children free of charge.

youngsters across England and Wales. The Compulsory Education Act of 1880 made attendance at elementary schools mandatory for children between the ages of seven and ten. In 1899 the age ceiling was raised to twelve. Over much of this period, the fee for a British elementary school was between one and four pence per week. By the century's final decade, it was free.

Working-Class Schooling

No one benefited more from educational reform than working- and lower-middle-class youngsters. Yet a working-class student's need to be educated continually clashed with the need to supplement the family income. In fact, few working-class children received more than two or three years of full-time schooling.

Most schools that served this class of students were operated by religious organizations. The National Society for Promoting Education of the Poor, supported by the Church of England, and the British and Foreign School Society were the two most successful. These societies required lessons based on Scriptures to be part of the curriculum. They were variously known as board schools, district schools, parish schools, village schools, voluntary schools, and national schools.

Smaller elementary schools usually had no more than one classroom to serve children between three and twelve years old. Students were instructed by an adult teacher and also a "pupil teacher," who was supervised by the adult. Pupil teachers were generally students who were at least thirteen years old, could read and write, and had a working knowledge of arithmetic and geography. One or two monitors also helped in the classroom. The monitors were younger students who performed tasks such as handing out paper and ink. Larger schools might have three classrooms: one for boys, one for girls, and one for the very young children, called "infants." There was often a separate adult female instructor for the girls.

For the poorest children, schools supported by charities were their only hope for a free education. Called "ragged schools," these institutions provided free meals and clothing to attract the youngsters into their classrooms. Their intentions were charitable, but they often carried a social stigma. "They sent all the poor little kids there and also they used to give breakfast tickets," one middle-class Bristol girl observed. "You had to be poor and ragged and have no boots, and you might stink."[55] Once there, the children were given their lessons by paid teachers and middle-class volunteers.

School Days

A typical day in a Victorian elementary school began at 9:00 A.M. and broke for lunch (usually called dinner) at 12:30. Classes resumed at 2:30 and ran to 4:30 P.M. Most students went

"The Inhospitable Regions of Examinations"

Academic examinations could be a welcome shortcut into an institution of higher learning for many eager scholars. For others, the tests were a source of anxiety and frustration. As a Victorian boy, future Prime Minister Winston Churchill fell into the second category, as he recounts in *My Early Life: 1874–1904*:

"I had scarcely passed my twelfth birthday when I entered the inhospitable regions of examinations, through which for the next seven years I was destined to journey. These examinations were a great trial to me. The subjects which were dearest to the examination were almost invariably those I fancied least. I would have liked to have been examined in history, poetry, and writing essays. The examiners, on the other hand, were partial to Latin and mathematics. . . . This was especially true of my Entrance Examination to Harrow. The Headmaster, Dr. Welldon, took a broad-minded view of my Latin prose. . . . This was the more remarkable, because I found I was unable to answer a single question in the Latin [portion of the exam]. I wrote my name at the top of the page. I wrote down the number of the question, "1". After much reflection I put a bracket around it thus, "(1)". But thereafter I could not think of anything connected with it that was either relevant or true. Incidentally, there arrived from nowhere in particular a blot [of ink] and several smudges. I gazed for two whole hours at this sad spectacle: and then the merciful ushers collected my piece of foolscap [a cheap grade of paper] with all the others and carried it up to the Headmaster's table. It was from these slender indications of scholarship that Dr. Welldon drew the conclusion that I was worthy to pass into Harrow."

home for dinner. Rural children had a longer walk home, so they usually brought dinner to school with them. In the poorer neighborhoods, local charities provided meals. The students did not attend school year-round. They were allowed two weeks' vacation at Christmas and one week at Easter. Summer vacation was three to four weeks long and ran from mid-July to mid-August.

The teaching was strict and impersonal. Reading, writing, and arithmetic were usually the only subjects taught. Students had to recite their lessons aloud, so classrooms were noisy. The smallest children were seated on long benches with shelves that served as desks. This arrangement limited the child's motions, making it difficult to shift position until the entire row did. Older children sat in groups or at separate desks. All students were obliged to sit still, stand when grown-ups entered the room, curtsy to the mistress (for girls), and line up before entering or exiting the schoolroom.

Discipline was swift and often severe. For minor infractions, a teacher rapped a student's knuckles with a wooden ruler. If that failed to discourage a child's undesirable behavior, such as talking out of turn or failing to follow instructions, he or she might be struck repeatedly on the buttocks or the backs of the thighs with a cane. While most children dreaded such punishments, others reacted more aggressively. A student in Bristol related his experience with one teacher who bullied him:

[He] was a big strapping man, he was over six foot tall. . . . I was sat in my desk one day with my copy book in front of me, writing what the teacher was dictating.

Young schoolchildren in a Birmingham classroom gather around their teachers to learn the alphabet, while others practice writing.

And I was conscious of [an ink] blot on the paper, but I couldn't do anything about it. But all at once . . . I felt a hand wham . . . right across my ear. Well, it stunned me for a minute, but I got out of my seat and I kicked him right in the shins. After that he sent me to the headmaster. But he [the headmaster] didn't do much about it . . . just reprimanded me.[56]

For the most serious offenses, the teacher recorded the erring student's name in the "punishment book." This volume held the record of a child's offenses over an extended period of time. Further infractions might earn the student a harder caning or even a bad reference when a future employer made inquiries at the school about hiring.

Education for the Middle Class

In Victoria's day, the organization of British educational institutions was very different from that of American schools. Victorian *public* schools were not paid for through state and local taxes. There were no school systems administered by elected officials. Instead, a public school's funding came principally from the sale of shares to public buyers. In some cases, an endowment from a wealthy individual or organization helped pay the bills.

Victorian *private* schools were institutions that were each owned and operated by a single proprietor. These schools varied greatly both in the number of students they enrolled and the types of courses they taught. Both public and private schools required some kind of student payment, at least until the 1870s when reforms demanded that schools be accessible to every child.

At the start of the industrial age in the mid-1700s, the grammar school had been providing the most democratic education. These classrooms featured the most thorough mix of social classes. Here, the tradesman's son sat next to the gentleman's son and enjoyed a kind of temporary equality. He might also gain the benefit of friendships with richer boys who could help his career later on. The usual subjects taught were Latin, Greek, and other classical subjects.

By Victoria's time, the classics were falling out of favor with students and parents alike. Courses in ancient languages like Latin and Greek began to seem too remote and lofty for the modern Victorian era. Gradually the sons of the gentry began attending public schools instead. At these exclusive schools, the gentry's sons could take more practical subjects such as arithmetic and English grammar, subjects needed to help them pass qualifying exams for upper-level schools. Eager to continue their contact with higher-class boys, the sons of the middle class followed suit.

A less expensive alternative to the public school was the private school. The size and curricula of private schools varied greatly. Historian Sally Mitchell provides examples of the wide range: "A widow who gave lessons in her dining room during the morning to five or six young children was considered to run a private school. A technical college that taught accounting, surveying and other vocational skills to youngsters between the ages of fourteen and eighteen was also considered a private school."[57]

The quality of private schools also varied sharply. In 1861 one education commission found:

[There is] distressing evidence as to the character of most of the private schools. . . . These were often taught by discharged servants or barmaids, outdoor paupers, small traders, washerwomen, cripples,

Perhaps the most famous of the English public schools was Rugby. Celebrated in the 1857 novel *Tom Brown's Schooldays* by former Rugby student Thomas Hughes, the school sought to plant the seeds of honesty, fair play, and "gentlemanly conduct" in its students. In one passage, the author describes the rigors, and disadvantages, of the school's "fourth form":

"The lower-fourth form, in which Tom found himself in the begining of the next half-year, was the largest form in the lower school, and numbered upwards of forty boys. Young gentlemen of all ages from nine to fifteen were to be found there, who expended such part of their energies as was devoted to Latin and Greek upon a book of [Roman historian] Livy, the 'Bucolics' of [Roman poet] Virgil, and the 'Hecuba' of [Greek dramatist] Euripides. . . . Then came the mass of the form, boys of eleven and twelve, the most mischievous and reck-less age of British youth, of whom East [Tom's friend] and Tom Brown were fair specimens. . . . The remainder of the form consisted of young prodigies of nine and ten, who were going up the school at the rate of a form a half-year, all boys' hands and wits being against them in their progress. . . . [They] were for ever being shoved down three or four places [in line for meals], their verses stolen, their books inked, their jackets whitened, and their lives otherwise made a burden to them. The lower-fourth, and all the forms below it, were heard in the great [larger] school . . . there, scattered about on the benches with dictionary and grammar, [the boys] hammered out their twenty lines of Virgil and Euripides in the midst of [babble]. The masters of the lower school walked up and down the great school together during this three-quarters of an hour, or sat in their desks reading or looking over copies, and kept just such order as was possible."

drunkards, consumptive and very aged persons. . . . Many of these schools were held in lofts, bedrooms, cellars, kitchens, shops, workshops, or other available but unsuitable places; where the children, generally more than infants, tumbled over one another like puppies in a kennel.[58]

"To Develop 'Character'"

When a boy of means reached the age of eight or nine, he was sent to a public school such as Eton, Harrow, or Rugby. This was not due to the schools' emphasis on Latin or Greek. "Most upper class boys were not sent to a public school to become scholars," writes Reader, "but to become reasonably well-educated men of the world, to meet other boys of their own kind and to develop 'character.'"[59] The public schools were also used to promote social contacts and sportsmanship through games such as cricket, football (soccer), and rowing. Instructors constantly stressed honesty, fairness, Christian virtues, and gentlemanly conduct to all students.

To run the daily business of public schools, headmasters employed the "monitorial system." This method placed the responsibility for discipline outside the classroom in the hands of the senior boys. Each new student arriving at the school was selected by an older boy to do chores and run errands for him. The idea was for the older student to provide friendship and guidance for the younger one, called the "fag" (with no sexual slur intended). Often this arrangement did little more than expose the new student to much bossing and verbal abuse. Most boys put up with this treatment for the sake of moving on with their education.

In Victorian Britain, the phrase "going to university" meant attending one of the two great English schools, Oxford or Cambridge. Oxford was a student's first choice for classical studies, while a young man attended Cambridge if he was strong in science or

mathematics. Both universities were composed of about twenty separate colleges. Each college had its own lecture halls, library, chapel, dining hall, and student lodgings. Each student had his own small suite of rooms with a study and bedroom.

The academic year was divided into three terms of about eight weeks each. Unlike American universities, Oxford and Cambridge did not have grades, regular exams, courses, or credits. Instead the student took on an individual, loosely organized regimen of reading and independent study. His only

The chapel building dominates King's College, Cambridge University. Most Victorian university students attended either Cambridge or Oxford University.

guidance came through regular meetings with a tutor. Otherwise, he was free to spend countless hours visiting or entertaining other students in his rooms discussing sports, politics, and less pressing matters, smoking, and playing cards. Only after ten terms of study did he put his knowledge to the test in a written and oral examination taken over several days. If his three or four years of self-directed study had educated him enough to pass, he received his degree.

Females in the Classroom

Victorian society saw little purpose in advanced education for girls. Many Victorians felt such schooling was pointless for someone whose future would be raising children and managing a household. The mind of a female, wrote essayist John Ruskin in 1865, "is not for invention or creation, but for sweet ordering, arrangements, and decision. . . . All such knowledge should be given her as may enable her to understand, and even to aid, the work of men."[60]

During their earliest years, children of both sexes were taught at home. As they grew older, however, the educational options for boys and girls changed dramatically. Author Judith Flanders explains the differences:

Boys left home early—they were mostly at school by the age of seven if school could be afforded. Even a day school ensured that boys spent much of their time with other boys; they became socialized early. The reverse was true of girls: the more prosperous the family, the less likely girls were to leave its shelter. . . . Girls who did not need to go out to work had no break to mark their passing from childhood to adolescence: they were often children until they married.[61]

However, a few privileged women, especially later during the Victorian era, were able to obtain an education. As with boys, the income level of a girl's parents determined the path of her education. A live-in governess might instruct the girls of a wealthy family until their late teens. Families who could not afford a governess instructed their female children at home until the age of nine or sometimes older. At this point, the girls began attending a private day school for the next few years. Adolescent girls from upper-middle- and upper-class families were usually sent away to boarding schools. Here they were instructed in languages, culture, the social graces, grooming, and good posture. Many private schools accepted only a small number of students; parents preferred institutions where their daughters received personal attention and close supervision.

Girls who had been tutored at home before entering private school sometimes held an advantage over other students. Such was the case for M. Vivian Hughes, who gives this account of her education:

In my twelfth year mother decided to send me to an "Establishment for Young Ladies" about a mile from home. . . . I was placed in the lowest class with three other little girls of my own age, who were reading aloud the story of Richard Arkwright. I say "reading," but unless I had had a book I should have understood not a word of their jerky mumblings. . . . When my turn came to read I held forth delightedly. Soon there was a whispered consultation with the Authorities, and I was removed then and there into a higher class.[62]

Like most students, Miss Hughes excelled in some subjects but struggled with

The Governess

"How delightful it would be to be a governess! To go out into the world; to enter upon a new life . . . to earn my own maintenance." So exults young Agnes, the heroine of Anne Brontë's 1847 novel *Agnes Grey*. Once a governess herself, Brontë drew upon personal experience to portray an enthusiastic young woman venturing out on her own.

By 1850, there were 21,000 governesses registered in England, a high number which kept pay low. The primary purpose of a governess was to teach the children of a middle- or upper-class family until they were old enough to attend school, a university, or to marry. Governesses worked either part-time or full-time.

A capable governess could teach English grammar and literature, history, geography, some mathematics, Greek, Latin, and French or German. She also gave instruction in vocal and instrumental music, dance, and drawing. Principally, she was expected to be a model of appropriate behavior to the children she taught and to guide their actions. This was easier said than done, as Anne Brontë's sister Charlotte discovered when she took a governess posi-

tion. Her account is quoted by Juliet Barker in *The Brontës:*

"The children are constantly with me, and more riotous, perverse, unmanageable cubs never grew. As for correcting them, I soon quickly found that was entirely out of the question: they are to do as they like. A complaint to [their mother] brings only black looks upon oneself, and unjust, partial excuses to screen the children."

Charlotte complained of the ceaseless chores assigned by her employer, who "overwhelms me with oceans of needlework, yards of cambric to hem, muslin night-caps to make and, above all things, dolls to dress."

A governess's position in the household was ambiguous. She was neither family nor a servant. She was an adult, yet she took her meals with the children and slept in the children's wing. Her salary was similar to that of the household servants, who often resented her for acting "better" than they. This dual perception sometimes made the position of governess difficult and lonely.

others. She received a painful reminder of this during the next day's lesson in arithmetic:

There followed something they called "mental arithmetic," of which I had never heard. The mistress stood up and gave forth sums from her head, and without any slate to work them out on the girls shouted the answers. One kind of sum smacked to me of black magic: "Twelve articles at fourpence three farthings each, how much altogether?" . . . A kind girl next

me told me in a hurried whisper to keep the pence and turn the farthings into threepences. But why? And what were the articles that one could buy so quickly? And supposing you only wanted ten?[63]

By midcentury an alternative to the small private schools became available to middle-class girls. At "collegiate schools," girls between ages twelve and eighteen received broader and more serious schooling. Such institutions as North London Collegiate School were large enough to organize students into separate classes according to age and ability. English literature and grammar, history, mathematics, biology, chemistry, political economy, and modern and classical languages made up the curriculum. As strict as this kind of school often was, Reader observes, "it did become possible for a few girls —at the start a very few—to get the same kind of intellectual training as their brothers, which was widely regarded as unladylike and probably bad for their health."[64]

The Limits of Learning

Yet the doors to the great males-only universities remained closed to young women throughout the Victorian era. In 1872 the first female students were at last permitted to take

Cambridge students protest the admission of women to the university in 1897. A separate women's college was opened at Cambridge during Victoria's reign.

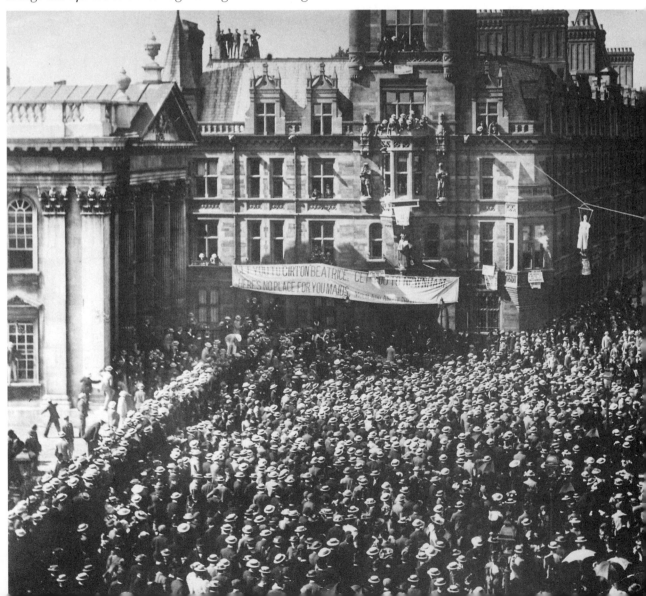

the entrance exams for Cambridge on an un-official basis, though the purpose of doing this is unclear since actual admission to the main school was still denied. Bowing to the growing demand for female education, however, both Cambridge and Oxford established separate women's colleges in the final quarter of the century. These institutions offered young women university-level instruction in literature, history, mathematics, and some of the sciences. Yet actual admission to exclusively male universities was not to happen during the reign of Victoria.

Despite these limits, education made remarkable gains during this era. The value of learning received greater attention than at any previous time in England's history. It began by breaking the barriers of class and ended with the first assaults on the barriers of gender. Young British women seeking greater educational opportunities would be able to pursue their dreams in the near future.

CHAPTER 6

"For Every Season and Occasion:" Social Life and Courtship

Like the people of any other era, Victorians felt the natural instinct for human companionship, both in groups and in couples. Whether in a modest town pub or a posh manor house, Britons followed a universal urge to gather with others of their own social level (if not higher). In many cases, loud music and inexpensive food were the ingredients for a good time. Quiet conversation and cultivated cuisine were better suited for other occasions. As the Victorian age drew on, the rise in the standard of living

This illustration of a Victorian pub in London depicts a lively scene of singing, dancing, and drinking ale.

for the middle class provided more time and money for their leisure pursuits. The style of a person's social life conformed to his or her station and pocketbook. Courtship was much the same way. The major difference lay in the fact that members of the lower classes had more freedom in one important personal passage: the ritual of securing a partner for life.

The English Pub

At the gatherings of the lower classes, alcohol was an ever-present ingredient of social interaction. Each year, Englishmen drank roughly thirty gallons of beer per capita. Fortunately, barley and the other ingredients for brewing malt, ale, and beer grew in abundance on the English countryside. Public houses, or pubs, were also plentiful across the land.

Pubs or taverns were often divided into two sections: a taproom on one side of the structure for the less prosperous drinkers, and the parlor on the other side for the wealthier part of society. The taproom was larger and might be outfitted with settles (wooden benches with high backs) and wooden tables near a large fireplace. The parlor was usually smaller but better furnished and adorned with pictures on the wall. Women and children were served in this section. Drinks were brought to the tables by a barmaid or a potboy. Named for the pots of beer or ale he served, the potboy also delivered beer to customers off the premises.

Workingmen who flocked to the pubs and gin houses after a hard day's labor received more than a few pots of beer. Some wished merely to erase the painful trials of poverty for an hour or two. Others enjoyed the conversation and companionship they found among their fellows—swapping tales, smoking their pipes, and singing the occasional drinking song. The larger establishments also featured a separate room for darts and billiards, or even a reading room stocked with newspapers. With these diversions, the pubs brought a measure of recreation and social interaction for those Englishmen who could afford nothing more.

Festivities and Footwork

While lower-class customers filled the public houses, the preferred social scene for many of the upper and middle class was often the formal dinner party. Besides an elegant table, flawless service, and exotic dishes, the occasion also provided its own style of after-dinner entertainment. The host family or specially selected guests performed in small-scale theatricals, each playing a different role. Especially popular were the *tableaux vivants*, a sort of freeze-frame portrayal of some dramatic or historical event. A curtain concealing a small, decorated backdrop complete with props was set up beforehand in a parlor or drawing room. When the curtain parted, one or more "actors" were revealed in dramatic poses which they held motionless—and silent—for as long as two or three hours. The costumes, props, and backdrop combined to heighten the effect of the scene: Cleopatra in a boat on the Nile River, a wood nymph picking flowers in the forest, or perhaps Joan of Arc poised for battle. In these motionless dramatizations, Victorian guests had a brief taste of the fantasy, history, and romance they enjoyed so much.

Dancing was one of the few social activities that everyone could enjoy, regardless of social level. For the lower classes, public dances called two penny hops attracted people of all ages. A fiddler usually provided the music. From half past eight until after

On Being Presented at Court

When a girl of the aristocracy was ready to enter fashionable society (and the marriage market), she was presented to the queen. Upper-middle-class girls were also eligible if their fathers were high-ranking naval or military officers, substantial country squires, or prominent members of the clergy or legal professions. Divorced women were not eligible until 1889. The event was regal, excruciatingly formal, and unforgettable to the young women lucky enough to be presented.

Queen Victoria held presentations several times during the social season at "drawing rooms" at St. James's or Buckingham palaces. In *Daily Life in Victorian England*, Sally Mitchell narrates a typical presentation:

"The girl being presented was generally about eighteen years of age. She wore a short-sleeved white dress with a long train [a length of fabric that trailed out behind the wearer]; her hair was decorated with a distinctive plume of white feathers. After her name was announced, she curtsied very low, kissed the queen's hand, and then backed out of the room. Girls about to be presented practiced carefully with their friends . . . nevertheless the prospect of walking backward in a low-cut dress with a train gave them nightmares."

After her presentation at court, the young woman began a dizzying circuit of parties and balls. These were designed to accomplish two things: to celebrate her entry into society and to launch the woman into the search for a suitable husband.

---

midnight, attendees danced the polka, country dances, and jigs.

Dances for the middle and upper classes were more elaborate affairs. Hosting a ball was an extremely important event for anyone high on the social ladder, or those still climbing. Hosts and hostesses followed strict rules of etiquette. A well-known self-help book titled *The Habits of Good Society* offered these words of advice:

Four musicians are enough for a private ball. . . . A piano and violin form the mainstay of the band; but if the room be large, a larger band may be introduced with great advantage. The dances should be arranged beforehand, and, for large balls, you should have printed a number of double cards, containing on the one side a list of the dances; on the other, blank spaces to be filled up by the names of partners. A small pencil should be attached to each card, which should be given to each guest in the cloak room. Every ball opens with a quadrille followed by a waltz. The number of the dances varies generally from eighteen to twenty-four, supper making a break after the fourteenth dance. . . . The Supper (quite separate from refreshments) hour in London is generally midnight, after which it goes on till the end of the ball.[65]

Guests at Victorian balls created an elegant tapestry of dances. The quadrille was a dance performed by four couples, and consisted of five figures, or sequences of movements, which the dancers could more or less walk through. More graceful and intimate was the waltz, a dance that allowed couples to dance independently of other pairs. Also popular was the polka, an energetic dance of Czechoslovakian origin (introduced to England in 1844) that involved rapid half steps. The galop was similar to the polka, only danced at a faster tempo. In this way, Victorians danced the night away.

Dressing for Society

No self-respecting Victorian would dream of appearing at a dance or any other social event without giving careful thought to what he or she would wear. "A well-dressed man," declared the anonymous author of *The Habits of Good Society,* "wants a different costume for every season and occasion; but if what he selects is simple rather than striking, he may appear in the same clothes as often as he likes."[66]

"Simple" was in. After the unnatural feel of the late-1700s and early-1800s clothing, Victorian men were ready for a change. The first three decades of the nineteenth century saw "small clothes," snug-fitting knee-length breeches, replaced by full-length trousers. The bold colors and rich fabrics of the previous century gave way to dark blue or brown buckskin, and finally to striped gray or solid black. So it would remain for the rest of the 1800s. For day wear, men discarded the cutaway dress coat with tails in the back and turned to the frock coat, a woolen garment cut to the knees all the way around.

"Shirts and underwear were of linen," Pool records. "It was cool, long wearing, and easily washed; in fact, for shirts it had snob appeal because it dirtied so quickly that if you could wear clean linen all the time you obviously had enough money to be a gentleman."[67] Full vests, called waistcoats, were worn between the shirt and the coat. Outfits might be brightened a little by silken cravats, broad short ties with a band that fastened around the stiff detachable collar. Most men favored black or brown boots that reached far up the calf. On the street, a tall silk hat marked the well-to-do gentleman; the rounded, low-crowned bowler was popular with the middle class.

Meanwhile, modesty was replacing daring in women's fashions. The high-waisted, low-necked dresses of the Regency era (the years 1820–1830 when George IV ruled) were out of style by 1830. The bodice (top portion) of the Victorian lady's outfit now fastened at the throat and fitted snugly at the waist. Sleeves were full-length. But the real change in women's fashions was the skirt. Early in Victoria's reign, the skirt was floor-length and full but used no padding to hold it out from the body. Gradually, skirt size swelled as women took to wearing as many as five or six layers of petticoats (underskirts) beneath their skirts. Multiple petticoats were soon replaced by a single, stiffer petticoat of linen and horsehair called crinoline. The 1850s brought women an alternative to crinoline—a bell-shaped frame of steel or whalebone hoops. Both the crinolines and the hoops made dresses so wide that climbing into carriages or even passing through doorways could be difficult. Furthermore, the broad sweep of the skirts sometimes came dangerously close to stoves and fireplaces.

The bustle helped alleviate some of these hazards. This style of underskirt padding eliminated fullness all around except the rear, where the skirt flared out sharply. The bustle remained popular through the 1860s, 1870s, and 1880s. By the turn of the century, however, skirts were generally unpadded, and sleeves were big and puffy. Beneath it all, women wore tightly laced corsets which gave them the smaller waist they coveted, but hampered both movement and breathing. All

homes in the West End. Here they slipped comfortably into the daily routines of urban society. According to Pool,

> In London, it was up early to go riding in Hyde Park, preferably on the sandy track known as Rotten Row (there was also the Ladies' Mile for the women), then home for breakfast. Shopping and paying bills for the ladies and making calls on those one knew extremely well came next. Then lunch, followed for men by the club—if they were not in Parliament . . .—while the ladies took to their carriages to leave [calling] cards and to pay still more calls. Dinner followed at around six or seven and in the evening there were soirees [parties or receptions] or the opera (dinner parties,

too, especially on the Wednesdays and Saturdays when there were no evening parliamentary sessions) and then balls or dances starting at ten or later that could go until three o'clock in the morning. [69]

For many in high society, the season did not really begin until Parliament returned from its Easter holiday. Then began an intense three months of balls, parties, concerts, and sporting events, in which the object was less to see than to be seen. The month of May saw the yearly exhibition at the Royal Academy of Arts. Later came two famous horse races, the Derby and the more exclusive race at Ascot. The Henley Regatta in July was the top sailing event of the season, while classic cricket matchups took place between Oxford

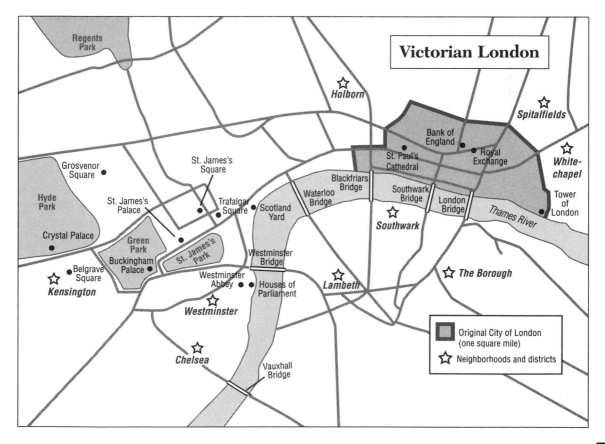

Tying the Knot

A Victorian couple's class dictated the style and circumstances of their wedding. Poor and working-class people dressed in their Sunday best and appeared at their local church before the regular morning service. Friends served as witnesses for the ceremony. Afterward, the wedding party went to the bride's house for breakfast. If the newlyweds could afford it, both would take a day off from work for the occasion. If not, the husband went to work while the bride worked at making their new home presentable.

The middle class followed a similar routine. The clothes, however, were nicer. The bride wore a dress made especially for the wedding, but serviceable for attending church and making social calls later. The usual colors were pastels or various hues in taffeta, velvet, and silk. The bride also wore a thin white veil over her head and shoulders. The groom wore a dark blue frock coat, a white waistcoat, and light-colored trousers. The shirt was white linen; the gloves were also white. The wedding party was larger and the newlyweds had time off from work to begin their marriage.

To make the betrothal legal, lower-class couples usually chose the least expensive option method, which was to "publish the banns." By this method, the parish rector or vicar made a public announcement of a couple's intent to marry during three consecutive Sunday services. As long as no one objected, the betrothed could marry in the next three months. Couples with a little more money could purchase a license from a clergyman which enabled them to get married in a parish where at least one of the couple lived. The most costly approach called for buying a "special" license which allowed the engaged parties to wed anywhere they chose. Those who were married outside the church secured a civil license.

A Victorian bride from a wealthy family cuts a lavishly decorated cake at her wedding celebration.

and Cambridge, and Harrow and Eton. In between were dozens of balls, scores of parties, and numerous dinners and breakfasts. It was high society in high gear, and it raged on until August 12 when both the season and Parliament came to a close.

Romance in a Fishbowl

Behind the whirlwind rounds of dinners, balls, and parties lay another, more serious objective. High-class social events provided many opportunities for young women and young men to meet. It was a so-called marriage market that was not taken lightly by those wanting to find a partner. Like hosting a ball or choosing the proper way to dress, courting followed distinct rules.

Unlike today, courtship in Victorian England was a very public matter. Middle-class parents and friends threw a "coming out" event for a young lady when she reached the age of seventeen or eighteen. Sometimes the occasion was a party or a private dance. Other girls "came out" at a county hunt ball or other public event. Whatever the event, this occasion was the young woman's formal introduction into society; it also served as a public announcement that she was eligible to begin courting. To emphasize the point, she began to dress and arrange her hair in a more grown-up fashion. For the aristocracy and upper middle class, the event was more regal: Girls came out at a presentation to the queen at court.

Once courting began, it was closely supervised by the young lady's mother, aunts, and grandmothers. They carefully screened interested males as to family connections, social position, and future prospects. (The parents of the young man also kept a close eye on the proceedings.) This is one reason why middle- and upper-class women usually married men they met inside the social circle of their own family. A courting couple never appeared in public alone. Whether they attended a party or a concert, or merely took an innocent walk in the park, they were chaperoned by at least one member of the woman's family. A man who paid a call on his sweetheart at her home seldom had a moment alone with her. Parents, siblings, or other relatives might remain in the parlor while the couple engaged in polite conversation on the sofa. Once the suitor became familiar to the family, he might accompany them to church or some other group event.

Sealing the Deal

A man could not propose marriage to a woman without contemplating certain factors first. "Because maintaining an acceptable middle-class life required a substantial investment in housing, furniture and servants, middle-class men tended not to marry until they were past thirty," Mitchell explains. "Engagements could last several years. It was not ethical for a man to pay serious attention to a woman unless his financial prospects would allow them to marry at some predictable date."[70]

Ordinarily, a middle- or upper-class man made the actual proposal to his beloved in person or by letter. If his proposal was accepted, the man would next approach the woman's father with his request. The father carefully considered the suitor's financial prospects before giving his consent. The couple then exchanged rings and lockets of hair. Since diamonds were not yet popular, the rings were set with pearls, turquoise or other stones, or nothing at all. Most engagements lasted between six and twelve months. Even with their intentions formally acknowledged, the betrothed couple was still expected to have a chaperone in public.

Marriage and Sex

Once the wedding was over, most Victorian couples entered a new frontier: the sexual side of their relationship. Sex was a major Victorian taboo. It was never discussed in polite company and seldom between husbands and wives. Women in particular often entered marriage largely ignorant of the subject. Society had other expectations of them. In 1857 Dr. William Acton outlined those expectations in *The Functions and Disorders of the Re-productive Organs*, excerpted here from J.B. Priestley's *Victoria's Heyday*.

"The best mothers, wives and managers of households, know little or nothing of sexual indulgences. Love of home, children, and domestic duties are the only passions they feel. As a general rule, a modest woman seldom desires any sexual gratification for herself. She submits to her husband, but only to please him."

Sex, women were told, was only for creating children. Any enjoyment of it was a betrayal of their status as wives and mothers. "The Victorians believed that passions ought to be under control," writes Esme Wingfield-Stratford in *Those Earnest Victorians*, "and that self-sacrifice is better than self-indulgence." If a Victorian wife felt any stirring of sexual desire, her options were to stifle the feeling or ignore it. Above all, she was to be faithful to her husband forever. Husbands, too, had requirements to fulfill. They were expected to remain true to their wives and uphold the sanctity of their marriages.

But rules and expectations could not always hold back human urges, even in the Victorian age. Husbands occasionally did stray from the path dictated by their wedding vows. They sometimes sought gratification in mistresses or prostitutes. In some cases, wives also took lovers. If and when the infidelity was revealed, shame and disgrace—at times in public view—often followed. Divorce or abandonment was sometimes the end result. For women, far more than men, the price of a ruined reputation could be devastating.

In the realm of courtship and marriage, the working class held what many considered an advantage. Young men and women who worked for a living had fewer rules of etiquette and propriety to contend with, and they were less beholden to their parents for financial support. For these reasons, working-class courtship was a less supervised affair than that of the upper classes. Courting was still conducted in public, but chaperones were not required. When the man's proposal was accepted by his intended bride, the couple did not need parental consent to announce their engagement. In these situations, less money meant more personal freedom.

Whatever their social or economic level, Victorian men and women continued the same basic social rituals that their ancestors had followed. Whether it was rowdy camaraderie in a public house or a sedate sit-down dinner, Victorians enjoyed the company of their peers. This was no less true of courtship. For in seeking suitable partners to marry, young men and women carried forward the traditions of their parents and grandparents to make their most important social connection.

CHAPTER 7

"To Amuse Our People:" Victorians at Leisure

When Victorians rested from their labors, they liked to fill their free time with amusements of all sorts. Outdoor competitions of speed and strength, indoor games of concentration and strategy, as well as music, novels, poetry, and the stage provided escape for Britons of all backgrounds. Some social observers saw a practical side to British recreations. "The more I look about me the more convinced I become," wrote Dickens to a friend in 1853, "that if we would only condescend to amuse our people a little more, they would drink and do worse a good deal less."[71]

Victorian Games

Victorian Britons drew a distinct line between "games" and "sports." Games were considered activities that were not too physically demanding and could be played by women and children, as well as men. The game of croquet, played outdoors with wooden mallets, wooden balls, and wire wickets, rose to great popularity in the 1850s. Archery and lawn tennis were as much social events as they were games. They gave young men and women of the middle and upper classes opportunities to meet and mix. Ice-skating, on the other hand, was an outdoor activity available to almost every Briton. All that was required was a frozen pond or river, and an inexpensive, or homemade, pair of skates.

For indoor amusement, Victorians frequently turned to chess, backgammon or cha-

rades. But their favorite diversions were card games. Whist, loo, quadrille, casino, faro, and patience (solitaire) were among the most popular. Some required a specified number of players, while others were "round games," where any number could play. These card games were generally played in the evenings, usually following the family dinner or a dinner party to round out a social evening.

Children also enjoyed games, indoor and outdoor, and often created their own playgrounds in the streets. As Alice Foley recalled near the end of the era,

Our street games were simple and traditional, but we found [them] wholly captivating. They came round with the seasons . . . shuttlecock and paddle; skipping rope; hoop-bowls; hop-flag and marbles. We small children loved the singing games, the quaint rhymes married to old ballad tunes and handed down from generation to generation. . . . In blossom time we organized May Queen processions; a tiny girl was chosen as queen to be adorned in odd finery, with a tinsel crown and a long curtain carried by her train-bearers. . . . Most of the older boys played football in the front street and were often chased by the local bobby [policeman]; at weekends they hung around the back streets or a gable-ends playing pitch-and-toss [a game where players throw coins at a selected target].[72]

Other youngsters found some of their diversions off the streets, especially if their parents were financially comfortable. One late Victorian son of a skilled artisan kept a detailed account of a typical week of activities and games:

> After tea I do my home-lessons. Then I go to a club at seven o'clock and play draughts [checkers], dominoes, gymnastics, etc. . . . from eight [o'clock] till about a quarter past I get errands for mother and at about half-past eight I go to bed. On Tuesday I go to a Band of Hope [temperance meeting] at half-past five and I come out at six, and if it is a wet week I go to a library on Monday dinner time and borrow a book and read it. On Wednesday I have a game with the boys in the street, and if it is a wet night I take in a friend of mine and play at ludo [a game using dice and wooden "counters" to advance around the board], draughts, dominoes, race games, etc. On Thursday I go to the Happy Evening [a recreational club] and play at hockey, painting, etc.[73]

Victorian Sports

In comparison to games, sports were viewed as serious contests, between two teams or two or more individual competitors, that were intense, physical, and generally be-

A Victorian family enjoys a rousing game of croquet, one of the most popular familial activities.

tween males. Football (known in the United States as soccer) and rowing were two of the most popular.

But no sport was more firmly rooted in English tradition than cricket. It was played chiefly by young men, although girls also played using a softer ball. Cricket requires two teams of eleven players each and an oval-shaped space in any sizable open area. A wicket is placed at each end of the field some 22 yards (20m) apart along the center line. The wickets consist of three stakes 28 inches (71cm) high forced into the ground in a line. Two "bails," or wooden sticks, are laid along the top grooves of each wicket. When a team is in the field, one of their players called a bowler delivers (or bowls) the ball from behind one wicket toward the other in an attempt to dislodge the bail. Defending the far wicket is a batsman from the opposing team. Wielding a flat-sided bat, he or she must try to defend the wicket and to hit the ball hard enough to score a run by running to the other wicket. An "innings" is over when ten batsmen have been put out.

The country-dwelling wealthy indulged their love of horsemanship and the thrill of the chase by joining in foxhunts. Enthusiasts were organized into local groups of like-minded sportsmen, called hunt clubs. Foxhunting was as much a social ritual as it was a sporting event. During the season, which began in November, hunt clubs sponsored a series of fine dinners, breakfasts, and balls for its members. Each club maintained a pack of hounds bred for hunting by a local "huntsman." The actual hunt was conducted in a large uninhabited section of an estate chosen for that purpose. The hounds were led to a "covert," a thick patch of shrubbery thought to be sheltering a fox. Catching the fox's scent, the hounds flushed out their quarry to the cry of "Tally-ho!" from the huntsman.

Playing Whist

Among the many card games enjoyed by Victorians during leisure time was the game of whist. An early version of bridge, whist was a favorite of Queen Victoria (although it has been said she did not play well). As described by Daniel Pool in *What Jane Austen Ate and Charles Dickens Knew*, whist is

"a game for two couples, the partners sitting opposite one another and each player being dealt thirteen cards. The first person puts down a card which the next person must match in suit if he can. Otherwise, he must play the trump suit [one of the four suits in the standard deck of cards which is selected to automatically defeat any other suit] or discard. The person who plays the highest trump or the highest card of the suit wins the trick [that round of play] and leads for the next trick. Points are won according to the number of tricks played and, sometimes, the number of honors held [the jack, queen, king, and ace of the trump suit. . . . A 'rubber' usually consists of the best two out of three games."

The excited pack pursued the fox across fields and streams, over or around fences, and through stretches of brush. The human participants followed at top speed astride their well-trained mounts, called hunters. When at last the hounds cornered and killed the fox, its tail and paws were sometimes awarded to selected riders as trophies. After 1860 more and more women joined the men in "riding to hounds." Their saddles were specially designed with a prong in front to permit riding sidesaddle.

An excited crowd waits for the start of the Derby Day horse race at Epsom Downs in 1890. Both the aristocracy and working class were avid horse racing fans.

Britons' fascination with horses popularized another sport. Like foxhunting, horse racing had a devoted following among the aristocracy. England's best-known race was the Derby, held each spring at Epsom Downs in the county of Surrey. The annual Derby Day was an unofficial public holiday. Its popularity created an unexpected social mix. More than the middle class, the working classes shared the aristocrats' enthusiasm for the "sport of kings." Both racing and boxing were mostly avoided by the middle class, which found the practice of betting on sports distasteful.

Musical Diversions

Of all the diversions in Victorian England, music was the most universal. Sentimental ballads, patriotic marches, choir music, sym-

phonies, and even opera were enjoyed by Britons from all walks of life. Author Ronald Pearsall describes the London music scene:

> There were barrel-organs and barrel-pianos in the streets grinding out their raucous melodies, there were German bands at every turn, and the spidery Victorian bandstands in recreation grounds and public parks are a memento to . . . the appeal of the military band. . . . There were dancing saloons, assemblies (the nearest approach to modern ballroom dancing), open air dancing at the various pleasure gardens such as Vauxhall, Cremone and Highbury Barn, promenade concerts . . . and hundreds of theatres presenting ballet, opera, burlesque, drama and music hall. [74]

Lower-class Englishmen loved burlesque. This was a loosely constructed program of singing, straight acting, dance, and comedy routines that poked fun at human frailties and institutions. Because of its occasionally racy subjects and bawdy humor, however, burlesque was considered too raw for respectable audiences.

Yet burlesque was the grandfather of the most enduring innovation in Victorian music, the comic operas of Gilbert and Sullivan. W.S. Gilbert was a failed barrister who became a successful writer for the humor magazine *Fun*. Arthur Sullivan was an acclaimed composer of oratorios, ballets, and hymns. Together they created a string of light operas that were outlandish in plot, yet sophisticated, witty, and supremely musical. *H.M.S. Pinafore*, *The Pirates of Penzance*, *The Mikado*, and many others featured familiar or exotic settings, colorful costumes, and memorable characters. Gilbert and Sullivan's greatest accomplishment was to make comic musicals not only respectable but admired worldwide.

But Victorians did not necessarily have to leave home to enjoy music. One reason was

The English Music Hall

For the Victorian workingman earning two pounds a week, there was no better evening's diversion than the music hall. The halls delivered a wide range of musical acts, food and drink, and fetching females. The acts were often loud, brash, colorful, and occasionally sentimental.

The halls themselves were often large and impressive. London patrons packed the older halls such as Canterbury Music Hall and the Grecian Saloon, each seating seven hundred patrons. The Grecian, writes Ronald Pearsall in *Victorian Popular Music*, featured "fireworks displays, open air concerts, dancing, fountains, cosmoramas [exhibits of scenes from around the world], grottoes [cavelike structures], [and] statuary." After midcentury, newer, larger halls rose five or six tiers above the orchestra pit and held up to three thousand spectators.

The variety of entertainment was remarkable. Audiences could enjoy programs of patriotic and comic songs, romantic ballads, farces, ventriloquism, gymnastics, popular dances, and the occasional ballet. Not even opera was too lofty for the halls' promoters. Since the traditional staging of operas in music halls was illegal, Charles Morton of the Canterbury once arranged his singers in rows on a bare stage to perform music from the opera *Faust*.

Celebrity vocalists nightly belted out the popular songs that were the staple of the music hall. "These singers," Pearsall points out, "relentlessly promoted . . . were paid enormous salaries. They frequently performed in several music halls a night, so great was the demand for their services." Dramas and farce made special demands on performers and stage managers, as Christopher Hibbert explains in *Gilbert & Sullivan and Their Victorian World*:

"Force and energy, bravura and panache [flair], were the qualities most admired; a performer who could not leap dramatically through a 'vampire trap' or fly gracefully to heaven on a wire would not last long in any company. Spectacle was the thing, and stage managers became adept at simulating thunderstorms, floods and cannon, dispatching characters offstage in flashes of colored smoke, bringing them on in a horse-drawn chariot, and lighting them up in a beam of light by burning a stick of lime in a gas jet."

A performance of acrobatics thrills patrons at a Victorian music hall. Such music halls offered a wide variety of entertainment.

the invention of the upright or "cottage" piano, a more affordable version of the grand piano. Another was a virtual explosion in the availability of sheet music. Popular ballads like "Home, Sweet Home" and classical favorites such as Beethoven's "Moonlight Sonata" were published in inexpensive editions, purchased by the thousands, and played at home. Sometimes called "drawing-room music," it quickly became a middle-class favorite for entertaining at home. Pearsall relates the usual after-dinner program:

> The ladies departed from the table, the port and claret [wines] went around twice . . .

coffee was called for and the men joined the ladies, who split up from a cluster and flew to the most interesting men. Conversation took place, and a lady emerged from the melee who had a voice or a touch. . . . [A] gentleman . . . escorted her to the piano to turn over the pages, and while she protested that she was so out of practice, she rapidly divested herself of gloves, fan and handkerchief. . . . Thus prepared the lady ran her hands up and down the keys with what was known as the "butterfly touch" as a signal for conversation to cease. . . . The audience stared at the ceiling, preparing their faces for melancholy or gaiety depending on the mood of the music. Execution was of less importance than touch or expression; a few wrong notes did not matter if the ones that were there were wrapped in sentiment.[75]

The British Periodicals

Music had certain advantages over other artistic forms of entertainment. Admission to music halls was cheap, sheet music was readily available, and people did not have to read or write to enjoy either one. But in the early days of the era, Victorians with literary interests were not so fortunate. "During the first half of the nineteenth century," writes Kristine Hughes, "reading was hardly a popular pursuit. Much of the population was unschooled and, more importantly, printed matter was too expensive for the common man."[76]

By the 1850s, however, public tastes were changing. Literacy had spread dramatically. Advances in technology and transportation made books and periodicals far more available. "The Victorians virtually invented mass literature," observes Mitchell. "High-speed presses, cheap wood-pulp paper, machines for typesetting, new means of reproducing illustrations, railways to send printed material all over the country . . . encouraged the publication of newspapers, magazines, and novels at every price and for every taste."[77] Not only were more individuals reading for pleasure, but reading as a family pastime gained wide popularity.

Monthly and weekly periodicals flourished. *Lloyd's Weekly Miscellany*, for example, featured illustrated news stories, spicy short fiction, humorous pieces, and the occasional fashion report. "Penny dreadfuls" such as *The Newgate Calendar* cost a penny and appealed to readers with a desire for "dread-

ful" crime and horror tales. Religious topics dominated the *Sunday School Penny Magazine*, and *The Teetotal Times* campaigned against the perils of alcohol. The household hints and romantic stories in "penny weeklies" such as the *Family Herald* were aimed at women. Teens and children read *The Girl's Own Paper* and *Good Words for the Young*.

Two publications dominated the popular literary scene. *The Strand* was the most renowned English illustrated magazine. Beginning in 1891, it further boosted its circulation by running the Sherlock Holmes detective stories written by Arthur Conan Doyle with drawings by Sidney Paget. A different reading audience turned to *Punch* magazine for its wit, satirical cartoons, and biting style of writing. "*Punch*," writes Professor Richard D. Altick, "was among the first and incomparably the greatest of the Victorian humorous journals, printing the work of many talented writers and artists and . . . exerting much influence on middle-class opinion."[78]

Chapter and Verse

The other great Victorian reading form was the novel, and Charles Dickens was its king. Born in 1812, Dickens poured his experiences as a destitute worker in a blacking factory, a crime reporter, and theater lover into his books and social criticisms. *Sketches by "Boz,"* a series of short pieces based on Dickens's observations of English life, was first published in 1836. This was soon followed by *The Pickwick Papers* (1837), *Oliver Twist* (1838), *David Copperfield* (1850), *Great Expectations* (1861), and others. Although many of his characters are haunted by tragedy and loss—several of his heroes are orphans—it was the humor and satire Dickens poured into his tales that endeared him to Victorians. Readers delighted in his young and innocent protagonists, his colorful and offbeat supporting characters, and his realistic, often impoverished settings. Dickens's stories were melodramatic and sentimental, tragic and hopeful—qualities that appealed strongly to Victorian readers.

Other novels dealt with issues that resonated with Victorian tastes, especially human relationships and the class system. Becky Sharp, the heroine of William Makepeace Thackeray's epic *Vanity Fair* (1847), struggles tirelessly to rise from her lower-class roots to reach the heights of society. In Thomas Hardy's *Far from the Madding Crowd* (1874), the poor shepherd Gabriel Oak vies for the af-

Charles Dickens remains the best-known Victorian novelist. His works portray Victorian life with humor and satire.

fections of his employer Bathsheba Everdene against a wealthy farmer and a dashing cavalry sergeant. *Jane Eyre* (1847) by Charlotte Brontë deals with a lonely young governess in love with her fiery employer Rochester, who is haunted by a terrible family secret.

Furthermore, the novelists engaged the younger readers as well. In his *The Jungle Book* (1894) and *The Second Jungle Book* (1895), India-born Rudyard Kipling enchanted youngsters with his tales of the boy Mowgli and his animal friends in the wilds of India. Lewis Carroll took children into the magical otherworld of the Cheshire Cat, the Mad Hatter, and the Queen of Hearts in *Alice's Adventures in Wonderland* (1865) and *Through the Looking-Glass* (1871). And once colored pictures could be printed more cheaply, such illustrators as Kate Greenaway made the children's picture book a staple of juvenile reading.

Readers who preferred poetry over prose were not disappointed. The Victorian period was a golden age for verse. Alfred Tennyson, Elizabeth Barrett Browning, William Wordsworth, Robert Browning, Matthew Arnold, and others were ardently plying their trade during Victoria's reign. Earlier poets such as John Keats, Percy Bysshe Shelley, and Lord Byron were gone, but their verses were as popular as ever. Compared to the price of a new novel, the cost of volumes of poetry was less expensive, making poetry more accessible to a lyric-hungry public.

The Play's the Thing

When Victorians preferred their stories presented live, there were plenty of options. The English stage was rich with entertainment at many different levels. At drama's most basic level was the slapstick mayhem of the "Punch

Popular though they were, novels were too costly for many working-class readers. To make book-length fiction affordable, publishers began releasing sections of novels in monthly parts. One of these serializations was Charles Dickens's *David Copperfield*, published in twenty segments beginning in May 1849. Sold in a paper wrapper at bookstores and newsstands, each illustrated section ran thirty-two pages and cost one shilling.

Another popular practice was to publish novels in installments in magazines. "Sensation novels" containing dark secrets, suspense, and exciting chases seemed tailor-made for this method. Two such books by popular author Wilkie Collins, *The Moonstone* and *The Woman in White*, first appeared in segments in the monthly periodical *All the Year Round* (edited by Dickens) in the early 1860s.

The serial was also ideally suited to a popular domestic activity, states Sally Mitchell in *Daily Life in Victorian England*.

"Reading aloud was customary during an evening at home. While most of the family occupied their hands with knitting or jigsaw puzzles and father relaxed in a comfortable chair, one person sat next to the only good lamp and read from a serialized novel or some other publication that would be interesting to both youngsters and adults."

Serial novelists were careful to end each section at a suspenseful point to encourage readers to buy the following issue. In both England and America, thousands of people eagerly discussed the latest serial with friends or neighbors while awaiting the next chapter.

In this age of sentiment and romance, emotional readers took their literature seriously. In one installment of Charles Dickens's *The Old Curiosity Shop* (1840), the author decided to kill off the popular character Little Nell. Readers were overwhelmed. On reading of Nell's death, grown men wept without shame alongside their wives and children. According to Peter Ackroyd in *Dickens*, one member of Parliament reportedly hurled his copy out the window of a railway car, crying, "He should not have killed her!" Countless readers wrote to Dickens begging him to bring Nell back to life. The author politely refused and *The Old Curiosity Shop* continued.

and Judy" shows. Often performed outdoors, these husband-and-wife puppet characters poked fun at marriage and authority figures. Working-class Britons flocked to see them.

Serious theater blossomed in the second half of the nineteenth century. British stages offered satire, light comedies, historical plays, and melodramas. It was this last dramatic form that Dickens and a friend set out to view one evening in 1850. He soon found that the play on the stage was not the only drama taking place in the house.

The Theatre was extremely full. The prices of admission were, to the boxes, a shilling; to the pit, sixpence; to the gallery, threepence. The gallery was of enormous dimensions . . . and overflowing with occupants . . . rising one above another, to the very door in the roof, all squeezed and jammed in. . . . The company in the pit were not very clean or sweet-savoured, but there were some good-humoured young mechanics among them, with their wives. These were generally

A crowd gathers outside the Theatre Royal Haymarket for a Punch and Judy show. These puppets were a favorite among the English working class.

accompanied by "the baby," insomuch that the pit was a perfect nursery. . . . There were a good many cold fried soles in the pit, besides; and a variety of flat stone bottles of all portable sizes. The audience in the boxes was of much the same character (babies and fish excepted) as the audience in the pit.[79]

For Victorians at all social levels, theater was a prime entertainment. In theaters plush or drab, audiences could enjoy the spectacle of such respected actors as Henry Irving and Ellen Terry performing the great plays of the nineteenth century and earlier. The 1880s and 1890s brought a fresh crop of young and daring playwrights. Oscar Wilde and George Bernard Shaw built lasting reputations for creating drama and comedy that sparkled, intrigued, and occasionally stung. In *Lady Windemere's Fan* (1893), Wilde explores the moral and social dilemmas that result when married couples are unfaithful. *The Importance of Being Earnest* (1899), a comedy about courting and false identities, relies more on Wilde's trademark lightning wit and intriguing characters to entertain.

Prostitution and women's roles are the subjects of George Bernard Shaw's controversial play *Mrs. Warren's Profession* (1898). Vivie,

Mrs. Warren's daughter, rebels on learning her mother's wealth comes from her houses of prostitution. Shocked and disillusioned, Vivie vows to live on her own as a "New Woman"— a modern, independent female. The drama is Shaw's attack on the male-dominated society that prevents women from being fairly paid for legitimate work. *Candida* (1898) is a domestic comedy in which the title character is the neglected wife of the Reverend Morell. When a young poet admits to Reverend Morell that he has fallen for Candida, she holds a kind of auction, forcing the two men to bid for her heart by proclaiming their love.

On the stage, in novels and magazines, in music, and in games and sports, Victorians sought relief from the stresses of their daily lives. Some of these diversions were physical in nature, some were rousing and funny, and others calm and uplifting. All provided a welcome, if temporary, escape from a world that could be harsh. For rich and poor alike, existence during the Victorian age was at best uncertain.

"Inward Peace and Inward Light:" Living, Dying, and Faith

Life during the reign of Queen Victoria was fragile. Diseases due to poor nutrition and unsanitary conditions were rampant. Childbirth was dangerous for both mother and child. Until the 1850s, the science of medicine had progressed little in centuries. Most remedies were homegrown and uncertain to cure. Victorians were only too well acquainted with illness, high infant mortality, and early death in adults. At the beginning of the period, the average life expectancy was around forty-two years old; at the end, it had only increased to forty-six.

For these and other reasons, many drew what comfort they could from their faith. The Victorians took their religion very seriously. In lives that were often filled with uncertainty and personal tragedy, men and women clung to their religious beliefs with grim determination; they taught their children to do the same. A popular poem of the day titled "Trust in God and Do the Right" by Presbyterian minister Norman Macleod reflected this devotion:

> Courage, brother! do not stumble
> Though thy path is dark as night;
> There's a star to guide the humble—
> Trust in God and do the right.
>
> Firmest rule, and safest guiding,
> Inward peace and inward light;
> Star upon our path abiding—
> Trust in God and do the right. [80]

But with the passing decades came new ideas, new sciences, and new interpretations of the Scriptures. The troubling questions that came with them weakened trust in traditional views of God. Spurred by these changes, the Victorian age of transition gradually became an age of doubt.

Medicine and Disease

Medical science was only emerging from its infancy during the early Victorian period. Advances were few and slow to take hold. Cholera and other intestinal ailments were commonly believed to be caused by "miasmas," or bad odors. Tuberculosis, the nineteenth century's leading killer, was thought to be hereditary. Meanwhile, the science of germs struggled for recognition and respect. Louis Pasteur's discovery of bacteria and its role in disease in 1861 was at first rejected by both scientists and the public. Near the end of the same decade, Joseph Lister demonstrated the value of carbolic acid in combating infections in hospitals and sickrooms. Yet it was not until the late 1880s that microorganisms were generally accepted as the cause of tuberculosis, cholera, and other diseases. The practice of scrubbing hands and boiling instruments by surgeons did not become routine until the 1890s.

Like other scientific advancements, medical improvements were slow to reach most people. Patent medicines were widely advertised but rarely effective. For the average family, medical care remained largely a hand-me-down affair. Most mothers or nannies still relied on centuries-old home remedies to treat their families' headaches, dog bites, nosebleeds, rheumatism, and broken bones. Their instruments and medicines were leeches, roots, boiled plants, animal fats, salt, olive oil, and vinegar. Few people trusted treatment in the crowded, unsanitary hospitals; the most momentous medical events in a Victorian's life took place at home.

Death in Birth

Throughout the century, many dangers accompanied childbirth. Kristine Hughes explains:

Childbirth in the nineteenth century was accomplished, as it had been for centuries, at home, with the help of a midwife. Midwives and "men midwives" had no formal training in delivery, usually learning their skill from family members. Though there were many who knew their craft well and carried it out with compassion, there had always been a high mortality rate due to ineptitude, unsanitary conditions and overdosing with both laudanum and opium, which were used to lessen the mother's pain and to quiet the cries of the child. [81]

The chances of a Victorian baby dying before his or her first birthday were ten to twelve times greater than they are in England in the twenty-first century. Even at the end of the

In this drawing from 1872, congregants in an Anglican church follow along in their prayer books as a priest leads them in worship.

Home Remedies

Many of the most popular treatments for life's daily ailments came not from the chemist's (pharmacist's) shop, but from grandmother and great-grandmother. Until the early twentieth century, home remedies handed down from one generation to the next served a family's medical needs. In *The Writer's Guide to Everyday Life in Regency and Victorian England: From 1811–1901,* Kristine Hughes has collected these and other widely used treatments:

"**To apply leeches:** . . . In placing them on the patient, put the mouth, which is in the tapering end of the body, against the patient. Place the leeches in a glass and turn it over upon the spot to be bitten. They must not be pulled off; when they have done their work they will fall off naturally. . . .

For the bite of a mad dog: Take a spoonful of common salt, add as much water as will make it damp and apply like a poultice every six hours, and it will be sure to stop the hydrophobia [effects of the rabies infection].

To stop a nosebleed: Put a nettle [a plant whose leaves are covered with hairs that secrete a stinging fluid] leaf upon the tongue and then press this against the roof of the mouth, or place a large flat key against the naked back.

Saline wash for headache: Take a half ounce of fine salt, four ounces each of vinegar and soft water, two ounces of whiskey or brandy and mix together until the salt is dissolved. This is a good cooling for headache and inflammation of the brain.

For the rheumatism: Take goose grease, melted with horse radish juice, mustard and turpentine. Shake till white and creamy, and spread on affected areas.

To cast a broken bone: Pick comfrey roots in March, when they are full of clear juice. . . . Grate up the roots, set the broken limb and use the mash [pulpy mass of roots] to cover the limb well. Make a joint in the cast to use when sawing off the cast later. The mash will be slow to set and will also promote healing."

---

era, infant mortality was high. In the upper classes alone, the rate was 136 deaths per 1,000 births in 1899. Among the poor, as many as 50 percent of infants died in their first twelve months of life. Working class women had little or no prenatal care. They were often poorly nourished and continued to toil at highly physical jobs throughout their pregnancies. The result was conditions such as rickets, a deformation of the bones caused by a lack of vitamin D, or anemia, a blood ailment brought about by lack of foods containing iron. These factors contributed to premature delivery and low-birth-weight babies.

The risk to the mother during childbirth was also great. In 1870 the rate of mothers' deaths was 1 in 204. Many married women gave birth to as many as ten or eleven babies over their childbearing years, severely weakening their bodies. An early death was the price thousands of women paid to the Victorian preference for large families.

From This World to the Next

Just as the beginning of life took place at home, so did the end. Excepting accident victims, most Victorians died in bed with loved ones nearby. Family members took turns sitting with the dying patient twenty-four hours a day. Once the person had died, a relative or a clergyman closed the deceased's eyes and placed a copper penny on each eyelid. This ritual ensured the lids would remain closed until the onset of rigor mortis (the stiffening of the muscles following death).

The body was then washed, dressed in a winding-sheet or a shroud, and laid out in a room apart from the others. Then a second watch began. As before, someone sat with the body around the clock until the burial, but for a different reason. In these days before Western culture knew of embalming, the fear of being buried alive was great. The person sitting with the body had to be watchful for any previously overlooked signs of life.

When it was time to bury the deceased, there was a strict etiquette to be followed. As Mitchell describes it:

> Funerals usually took place in the morning. Among the gentry and prosperous middle classes, the coach was draped in black, and the horses wore black plumes. The coffin was carried by the family's

Young children get their first glimpse of their baby sister. Infant mortality among Victorian babies was exceptionally high.

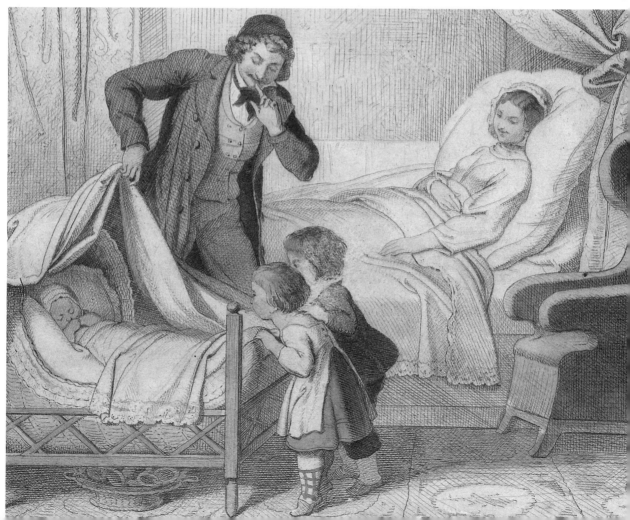

men-servants and by the undertaker's men. Male friends or hired mourners called "mutes" walked alongside. Sometimes they carried the heavy black pall [a cover, usually velvet] that was draped over the coffin. Everyone attending the funeral wore black garments made of wool and crepe. Men wore black gloves; flowing bands of black cloth known as "weepers" were tied around their hats. [82]

Walking funerals were the norm for the working class. Unable to afford a carriage or hired mourners, the deceased's family did almost everything themselves. Four friends bore the coffin on their shoulders, while four others walked alongside to relieve them. The family walked behind the coffin, and the remaining mourners followed. At the end of the burial, close friends and relatives shared a large meal at the family home or at the local tavern.

The mourning began in earnest after the funeral. Mourners of all classes continued wearing black to publicly acknowledge their private grief. While a widower needed only to wear a black armband, a widow was expected to modify her entire wardrobe. The

The Rituals of Death

The Victorians held the dead in great respect and observed a number of traditional death rituals. Their beliefs on the subject, however, were not without a tinge of superstition. In his book *London and Londoners in the 1850s and 1860s*, Victorian author A.R. Bennet outlines the aftermath of a death. It is excerpted here from Kristine Hughes, *The Writer's Guide to Everyday Life in Regency and Victorian England: From 1811–1901*.

"As soon as a death occurred in a house, the entire household, including the servants, went into deepest mourning. The house blinds were drawn, the clocks stopped and the mirrors covered to prevent the decedent's spirit from becoming trapped inside them. Whilst it was considered unwise to ever lock the door of a room containing a corpse, in case the spirit became trapped inside, the body was never to be left alone between the time of death and burial, and was watched over at all times. Candles were kept burning near the corpse and a plate of salt was sometimes placed on its chest to both delay corruption and ward off evil. It was considered the height of bad manners for any visitor to the house not to at least view the body, no matter how casual the acquaintance."

Even the tolling of the church bell for the deceased followed a prescribed sequence. According to Hughes,

"In rural communities, the ringing of a 'passing bell' in the parish church signaled that someone lay on his or her deathbed. The bell tolled six times for a woman, nine for a man, followed by a peal for each year of the dying person's life. When the body was later brought to the grave for burial, an additional toll, the death knell, was sounded to inform the parish that the deceased had been safely laid to rest."

With this simple system, the church and the bereft family could share with the community the grim progress of committing the deceased to the earth.

length of time for wearing black varied for working people. For the upper classes, however, the roles of mourning were much more severe. The 1888 manual *Manners and Rules of Good Society* laid out the rules:

> The regulation period for a widow's mourning is two years. Of this period crepe should be worn for one year and nine months— for the first twelve months the dress should be entirely covered with crepe, and for the remaining three months trimmed with crepe. During the last three months black without crepe should be worn. After two years, half-mourning is prescribed. . . . The widow's cap should be worn for a year and a day. [83]

On the death of her husband, Prince Albert, in 1861, Victoria donned the customary widow's "weeds" or mourning garments. Unlike most widows of her time, she continued wearing them for the rest of her life, a full forty years.

The Church in Daily Life

In the midst of suffering and loss, most Victorians turned to a higher power for comfort and meaning. For many, the trauma of loss and the weight of grief could be eased only in the quiet of the church and in the pages of the Scriptures. Victoria's England, in fact, was a nation of churchgoers. A national survey taken one Sunday in March 1851 indicated that 60 percent of the population was attending church. England had no shortage of houses of worship and offered a variety of denominations.

The most dominant of these was the Church of England, or Anglican Church. It had been formed in 1534 when King Henry VIII severed ties with the papacy. Originally Catholic, the Church of England had taken on many Protestant values and customs. Three centuries later, English Catholics were still scorned by the overwhelming number of their Protestant countrymen. In the mid-1800s, Catholics made up only 4 percent of the Victorian faithful; Anglicans accounted for not quite half. Yet the Church of England wielded wide-ranging power in nineteenth-century Britain. As the official state church, it enjoyed legal control over marriages, divorces, and wills. It also had several levels that referred to the formality of ritual and strictness of belief of its followers. At one level—the so-called High Church—it emphasized the most formal approach to worship through its elaborate ceremonies. At the next level, the Broad Church members were of a more tolerant and liberal bent, and remained more accepting of the advances of modern science. Advocates of the Low Church, called evangelicals, believed in individual salvation, a strict and pious lifestyle, and performing good works. The evangelicals' zeal for helping others led to many of the nineteenth century's most significant reforms: the abolition of slavery, flogging, and public hangings; the regulation of work hours; the establishment of asylums and orphanages; and the creation of schools. Among the most enduring charitable organizations they established were the Society for the Prevention of Cruelty to Animals, the Children's Aid Society, Women's Universal Alliance of Peace, and the Young Men's Christian Association (YMCA).

Many Protestants were not Anglicans. These non-Anglican denominations rejected the Thirty-nine Articles of Faith, which had outlined Anglican doctrine following England's split with Rome in the sixteenth century. Because they refused to conform to the

The words above the image read:
"Come . unto . me . all . ye . that . Labour! . and . are . heavy . laden . and . I . will . give . you . Rest ."

"The . Eternal . God . is . thy . Refuge . and . underneath . are . the . Everlasting . arms ."

In this 1864 illustration, a large group of homeless poor in London seek refuge for the night inside a church.

full creed of the Anglican Church, they were called Nonconformists or Dissenters. From their viewpoint, a person should be able to have a direct relationship with God. Forgiveness for sins should come from him without the intervention of a priest. Denominations practicing this type of faith included Methodists, Presbyterians, Baptists, Unitarians, Congregationalists, and Quakers. Together they composed 49 percent of all churchgoing Victorians.

Church for the Nonconformist denominations was more than a series of weekly activities and services; it was the centerpiece of their daily lives. Many lower–middle-class workers found many of their other needs met by their churches. In Sunday school, their children were taught to read. The chapel choirs, study groups, and mission societies provided recreation. Working men who took on roles as deacons and lay preachers enjoyed a measure of authority and respect they would otherwise have missed.

Remember the Sabbath Day

The centerpiece of the church week for any denomination was the Sunday service. Most Victorian Christians were strict in their observance of the sanctity of the Sabbath. The day was nearly devoid of anything secular. The majority of families attended at least two Sunday church services, one at 10:00 A.M. and another in midafternoon or early evening. They might also go to midweek prayer meetings or Bible study groups. In the Church of England, well-off young women were expected to teach children in Sunday school. In the dissenting churches, young males often gave religious instruction to members of all ages.

Even in church, social position was evident. The families of the clergymen and village squire or other dignitaries were seated at the front of the sanctuary. They might enjoy the extra privilege of sitting in a box pew with high sides, doors, and plush cushions. In the winter months, charcoal braziers gave warmth to their pews. Other notable families could rent their own pews behind those of the dignitaries. The poor sat at the rear of the chapel in free seating.

Sunday services were not brief. The involved rituals and lengthy sermons could test the patience of the most devout Christian, especially the youngsters. M. Vivian Hughes had vivid recollections of sitting in church:

My back still aches in memory of those long services. Nothing was spared us—the whole of the "Dearly Beloved," never an omission of the Litany, always the full ante-Communion Service, involving a sermon of unbelievable length. The seats and kneeling-boards were constructed for grownups (and not too comfortable for *them*), and a child had the greatest difficulty in keeping an upright position.

A Parish Clergyman

The clergyman of a church parish was the local religious leader of an English community. His duties were varied and often well rewarded, as Daniel Pool relates in *What Jane Austen Ate and Charles Dickens Knew:*

"The local representative of the church was the parish 'priest,' as the vicar, rector, or perpetual curate of a parish was known. He conducted the services in the local parish church, tended to the sick, officiated at baptisms, christenings, funerals and so on. His post was officially known as a 'benifice,' or a 'living' and it could be used to maintain a handsome lifestyle. The minister was entitled to all or part of the local tithes, the mandatory annual payments by parishioners to sustain the church, which . . . consisted of one-tenth of the farm produce in the area."

In poorer parishes, a clergyman's income might be much more modest. He was known as the "rector" or the "vicar," depending on the way the parish was funded. In some parishes the clergyman hired a "curate"—a clergyman without his own "living"—to help out with the duties required by the parish.

A clergyman's chief assistant was his wife. She often recruited women of the gentry and middle class to help with the task of visiting the poor and the working class in the parish. These "visitors" went to a parishioner's home, asked after the family's welfare, and gave advice. If a family member was ill, the visiting women helped supply food or arranged for him to get medical care. They provided blankets in the winter, and found clothing for newborn babies. If the need of a parish family was a spiritual one, the visitors read aloud a prayer or verses from Scripture. They might also leave a religious pamphlet for the adults or a moral story for the children.

. . . The sermons were usually stiff with learning and far over our heads. After one on Solomon's vision, I asked [my brother] Barnholt on the way home whether *he* would have chosen wisdom if he had been Solomon. "Oh, no," said he, "I've got enough of that. I should have asked for a new cricket-bat."[84]

The time after church was not always much better. Hughes continues:

The afternoons hung heavy. It seemed to be always three o'clock. All amusements, as well as work, were forbidden. It was a real privation not to be allowed to draw and paint. . . . Naturally our main stand-by was reading, but here again our field was limited by mother's tedious notions of what was appropriate for Sunday. *Tom Brown*, *Robinson Crusoe*, Hans Christian Andersen's *Tales*, and *Pilgrim's Progress* were permitted, but not the *Arabian Nights*, or Walter Scott, or indeed any novel.[85]

No housework, not even cooking, was allowed on the Sabbath. As a result, dinner tables were laid out with cold meats, bread, and cheese. Finally, there was always one final Sunday diversion—the second church service.

Challenged Beliefs

Beyond the Sunday services, new challenges awaited the faithful. The powerful changes sweeping the nineteenth century were reshaping Victorian thinking. Religion was not spared. Cherished beliefs about the relationship of humankind to God were being rocked by new views of the Scriptures and fresh discoveries in the natural sciences.

During the mid-1800s, a growing number of biblical scholars came to question the reliability of historical data contained in the Old Testament. In a wave of new interpretations, Biblical researchers began to see the Old Testament as a collection of genealogies, tribal histories, folk tales, and biographies. But scholars wondered if it was inspired by God or written by ordinary men without divine guidance. The maturing science of geology heaped more doubt on the debate. Traditional interpretations of the Bible suggested the earth was no more than six thousand years old. Yet recent discoveries of fossils preserved in rock and even the bones of dinosaurs indicated that the earth must be thousands or even millions of years old. For the first time, many educated Victorians began to feel the dark stirrings of uncertainty.

Then in 1859, a self-taught scientist named Charles Darwin published a treatise titled *On the Origin of the Species by Means of Natural Selection*. In its pages, Darwin declared that the earth's animals did not necessarily exist in their original states. If changes in a creature's environment threatened its existence, the creature's body altered, or evolved, to adapt to the threat. This process of evolution might take millions of years to complete. Most importantly, *man* as well as animals had undergone these changes. Darwin was not the first scientist to put forward the idea of evolution, but he was the first to utilize years of observation and study to devise a theory to explain natural selection or "survival of the fittest."

Religious leaders were outraged by the theories of Darwin and others. Their radical ideas seemed to call into question the time-honored teachings of the Bible, particularly the story of creation as recounted in the book of Genesis. If the earth and its occupants had not been created in seven days, had there really been an Adam and Eve? If not, then what about the Garden of Eden, or the Temptation, or the Fall of Man? Without the concepts of original sin and redemption, the whole litany of Christian beliefs seemed shadowed in doubt.

In response, many churches merely rejected evolutionary theories and held fast to their traditional beliefs. Others modified some of their teachings and remained true to the others. But for a number of Victorian intellectuals and clergymen, the religious foundation of their lives was badly shaken. Some ministers gave up their calling, while others continued to preach without the certainty

Charles Darwin shook the foundation of Victorian religious beliefs with his theory of evolution.

they once enjoyed. But little of this had any immediate effect on ordinary Victorian churchgoers. To them, the high-flown theories of scientists seemed distant and vague. It is likely that their religious beliefs were not immediately affected by the controversy that raged among more educated men. The everyday Victorian remained reassured and comforted by a relationship with his maker that was slow to change.

The Spirit of the Age

Throughout Victoria's reign, men and women struggled to find a balance between the old and the new. They searched for the line between the beliefs that comforted them and the ideas that challenged them. Evans and Evans describe the dual nature of the nineteenth-century Briton:

> The Victorian was an idealist—but he was also a realist. He was a dreamer — but his favorite dreams were those which could be made true. He was a believer—but he believed most strongly where he could feel solid fact beneath his feet. That way, nobody could make a fool of him; for to the Victorian, the highest praise was that he was nobody's fool. [86]

On January 22, 1901, the woman who lent her name to a long and turbulent era died peacefully in her bed at Osborne House on the Isle of Wight. Prince Albert had passed forty years earlier; their son Albert Edward, now sixty himself, prepared to take the throne. Victoria's reign had lasted sixty-four years, a span that took England from the days of the early railroads to the days of the early motorcars.

The years in between had seen unprecedented technological, social, economic and political change.

The Victorian period saw England at the peak of its wealth and world leadership in trade, industry, technology, and military power. The era witnessed the nation's control of one-quarter of the world's territories and its reign over one-fourth of its population. But by Victoria's death, England's leadership in global trade and industry was losing ground to the United States and Germany. The piece-by-piece loss of its colonial possessions chipped away at the empire. The prestige of the monarchy itself was in decline.

Yet the Victorian era had left an indelible mark on the nation. Despite the gradual eroding of England's worldwide domination, the ethics of family life, hard work and optimism remained. The Englishman's pride in his country and confidence in facing the future was stronger than ever. Although the age of Victoria was ending, Britons would carry these values forward into the new century.

Notes

Introduction: The Nineteenth Century and Change

1. Quoted in Walter E. Houghton, *The Victorian Frame of Mind, 1830–1870*. New Haven, CT: Yale University Press, 1957, p. 4.
2. Quoted in Nicole Roth, "The Sun Never Sets on the British Empire," Virginia Tech, Department of English. www.athena.english.vt.edu/~jmooney/3044main/syllabus.html. (Quotation originally published in Christopher North, Noctes Ambrosianae, *Blackwood's*, 1829).
3. Quoted in Sally Mitchell, *Victorian Britain: An Encyclopedia*. New York: Garland, 1998, p. 280.

Chapter 1: "The Darkest Shadow:" Work and the Lower Classes

4. Quoted in Gertrude Himmelfarb, *The Idea of Poverty: England in the Early Industrial Age*. New York: Vintage, 1985, p. 198.
5. Kristine Hughes, *The Writer's Guide to Everyday Life in Regency and Victorian England: From 1811–1901*. Cincinnati: Writer's Digest, 1998, p. 115.
6. Daniel Pool, *What Jane Austen Ate and Charles Dickens Knew: From Fox Hunting to Whist—the Facts of Daily Life in Nineteenth-Century England*. New York: Touchstone, 1993, p. 154.
7. W.J. Reader, *Victorian England*. London: B.T. Batsford, 1964, p. 38.
8. Gillian Avery, *Victorian People: In Life and Literature*. New York: Holt, Rinehart and Winston, 1970, p. 91.
9. Reader, *Victorian England*, p. 49.
10. Kristine Hughes, *The Writer's Guide to Everyday Life in Regency and Victorian England*, p. 120.
11. Quoted in Reader, *Victorian England*, pp. 48–49.
12. Quoted in Jeffrey Meyers, *D.H. Lawrence: A Biography*. New York: Knopf, 1990, p. 8.
13. J.F.C. Harrison, *The Early Victorians, 1832–1851*. New York: Praeger, 1971, pp. 41–42.
14. Meyers, *D.H. Lawrence*, p. 6.
15. Clarice Swisher, ed. *Victorian England*. San Diego, CA: Greenhaven Press, 2000, p. 110.
16. Quoted in Mary Ann Witt et al., *The Humanities: Cultural Roots and Continuities*, 2nd ed., vol. 2, *The Humanities and the Modern World*, Boston: Houghton Mifflin, 1985, p. 113.
17. Quoted in Reader, *Victorian England*, p. 73.
18. Nicolas Bentley, *The Victorian Scene: A Picture Book of the Period, 1837–1901*. London: George Weidenfeld & Nicolson, 1968, p. 102.
19. Henry Mayhew, *Selections from London Labor and the London Poor*, quoted in Avery, *Victorian People*, p. 219.
20. Harrison, *The Early Victorians*, pp. 45–46.
21. Hannah Cullwick, *The Diaries of Hannah Cullwick, Victorian Maidservant*, ed. Liz Stanley. New Brunswick, NJ: Rutgers University Press, 1984, p. 68.

Chapter 2: "Seize the Prizes:" Work and the Middle Classes

22. Hilary Evans and Mary Evans, *The Victorians: At Home and at Work*. New York: Arco, 1973, p. 14.

23. Reader, *Victorian England*, pp. 114–115.
24. Quoted in Kristine Hughes, *The Writer's Guide to Everyday Life in Regency and Victorian England*, pp. 156–57.
25. Pool, *What Jane Austen Ate and Charles Dickens Knew*, p. 108.
26. Charles Dickens, *Selected Journalism, 1850–1870*, ed. David Pascoe. London: Penguin, 1997, p. 246.
27. M. Jeanne Peterson, *The Medical Profession in Mid-Victorian London*. Berkeley: University of California Press, 1978, p. 5.
28. Pool, *What Jane Austen Ate and Charles Dickens Knew*, pp. 250–52.
29. Quoted in Gordon Winter, *Past Positive: London's Social History Recorded in Photographs*. London: Chatto & Windus, 1971, p. 68.
30. Pool, *What Jane Austen Ate and Charles Dickens Knew*, p. 131.
31. Pool, *What Jane Austen Ate and Charles Dickens Knew*, p. 133.
32. Evans and Evans, *The Victorians: At Home and at Work*, p. 14.

Chapter 3: "Unfit for People:" The Lower Classes at Home

33. Reader, *Victorian England*, p. 64.
34. Quoted in Harrison, *The Early Victorians*, p. 58.
35. Quoted in Reader, *Victorian England*, p. 47.
36. Quoted in Christopher Hibbert, *The English: A Social History, 1066–1945*. New York: W.W. Norton, 1987, p. 573.
37. Quoted in Reader, *Victorian England*, p. 80.
38. Charles Dickens, *Selected Journalism, 1850–1870*, p. 301.
39. Quoted in Henry Mayhew, *Selections from London Labor and the London Poor*, ed. John L. Bradley. London: Oxford University Press, 1965, pp. 56–57.
40. Quoted in Harrison, *The Early Victorians*, pp. 27–28.
41. Pool, *What Jane Austen Ate and Charles Dickens Knew*, p. 204.
42. Quoted in Reader, *Victorian England*, p. 46.

Chapter 4: "The Crystal of Society:" Home for the Middle and Upper Classes

43. Quoted in Kate Flint, introduction to *Hard Times*, by Charles Dickens. London: Penguin, 2003, p. xxvii.
44. Charles Petrie, *The Victorians*. London: Eyre & Spottiswoode, 1960, p. 131.
45. Petrie, *The Victorians*, p. 132.
46. Isabella Beeton, *The Book of Household Management*, 1861. Facsimile edition. New York: Farrar, Straus & Giroux, 1969, p. 1.
47. Winston Churchill, *My Early Life: 1874–1904*. Introduction by William Manchester. New York: Touchstone, 1996, p. 5.
48. Quoted in Anthony Burton, "Small Adults," in *The Victorian Vision: Inventing New Britain*, ed. John M. Mackenzie. London: V & A, 2001, p. 88.
49. Laura Wilson, *Daily Life in a Victorian House*. Washington, DC: The Preservation Press (National Trust for Historic Preservation), 1993, p. 26.
50. Quoted in C.O. Peel, *A Hundred Wonderful Years, 1820–1920: Social Domestic Life of a Century*. New York: Dodd, Mead, 1927, p. 157.
51. Quoted in Peel, *A Hundred Wonderful Years, 1820–1920*, p. 111.
52. Beeton, *The Book of Household Management*, p. 952.
53. Kristine Hughes, *The Writer's Guide to Everyday Life in Regency and Victorian England*, p. 194.

Chapter 5: "Her Noblest Wealth:" Education in Victorian England

54. Wordsworth, *The Excursion*, bk. 9, lines 294–95. www.bartleby.com/145/ww406.html.
55. Pamela Horn, *The Victorian Town Child*. Washington Square: New York University Press, 1997, p. 76.
56. Quoted in Horn, *The Victorian Town Child*, pp. 9–10.
57. Sally Mitchell, *Daily Life in Victorian England*. Westport, CT: Greenwood, 1996, pp. 165–66.
58. Quoted in Peel, *A Hundred Wonderful Years, 1820–1920*, p. 22.
59. Reader, *Victorian England*, p. 22.
60. Judith Flanders, *Inside the Victorian Home: A Portrait of Domestic Life in Victorian England*. New York: W.W. Norton, 2004, p. 90.
61. Quoted in Flanders, *Inside the Victorian Home*, p. 89.
62. M. Vivian Hughes, *A London Girl of the 1880s*. London: Oxford University Press, 1936, pp. 69–70.
63. Hughes, *A London Girl of the 1880s*, p. 71.
64. Reader, *Victorian England*, p. 124.

Chapter 6: "For Every Season and Occasion:" Social Life and Courtship

65. Quoted in Kristine Hughes, *The Writer's Guide to Everyday Life in Regency and Victorian England*, p. 204.
66. Quoted in Kristine Hughes, *The Writer's Guide to Everyday Life in Regency and Victorian England*, p. 53.
67. Pool, *What Jane Austen Ate and Charles Dickens Knew*, p. 217.
68. Pool, *What Jane Austen Ate and Charles Dickens Knew*, pp. 50–51.
69. Pool, *What Jane Austen Ate and Charles Dickens Knew*, pp. 51–52.

70. Mitchell, *Daily Life in Victorian England*, p. 156.

Chapter 7: "To Amuse Our People:" Victorians at Leisure

71. Dickens, *Selected Journalism. 1850–1870*, p. 499.
72. Quoted in Horn, *The Victorian Town Child*, p. 153.
73. Quoted in Horn, *The Victorian Town Child*, p. 66.
74. Ronald Pearsall, *Victorian Popular Music*. Detroit, MI: Gale Research, 1973, pp. 13–14.
75. Pearsall, *Victorian Popular Music*, p. 88.
76. Kristine Hughes, *The Writer's Guide to Everyday Life in Regency and Victorian England*, p. 128.
77. Mitchell, *Daily Life in Victorian England*, p. 233.
78. Richard D. Altick, *Victorian People and Ideas*, New York: W.W. Norton, 1973, p. 67.
79. Dickens, *Selected Journalism, 1850–1870*, p. 501.

Chapter 8: "Inward Peace and Inward Light:" Living, Dying, and Faith

80. Quoted in Mitchell, *Daily Life in Victorian England*, pp. 251–52.
81. Kristine Hughes, *The Writer's Guide to Everyday Life in Regency and Victorian England*, p. 66.
82. Mitchell, *Daily Life in Victorian England*, p. 161.
83. Quoted in Mitchell, *Daily Life in Victorian England*, p. 163.
84. Hughes, *A London Girl of the 1880s*, pp. 81–82, 85.
85. Hughes, *A London Girl of the 1880s*, pp. 85–86.
86. Evans and Evans, *The Victorians*, p. 91.

For Further Reading

Victorian Novels

Charlotte Brontë, *Jane Eyre*. New York: Modern Library Classics, 2000. This is the story of the shy orphan girl who becomes governess to the daughter of the fiery and mysterious Rochester. A perennially popular tale of mystery and dark family secrets, the novel has been made into several movies, television adaptations, and a stage musical.

Emily Brontë, *Wuthering Heights*. New York: Washington Square, 1968. A sister of Charlotte Brontë, Emily's only novel became a classic. Using the rugged moors of the north of England as a backdrop, Brontë tells the dark love story of the beautiful Catherine and the brooding Heathcliff, and of the fate of the ill-starred Earnshaw and Linton families.

Charles Dickens, *David Copperfield*. New York: Penguin Classics, 2003. Considered by some to be Dickens's greatest work, this 1850 novel is perhaps his most autobiographical as well. Filled with many of Dickens's most memorable characters—the Micawbers, Clara Peggotty, Miss Trotwood, Uriah Heep—*David Copperfield* is the story of a boy's rise to manhood in Victorian England.

Charles Dickens, *Oliver Twist*. New York: Penguin Classics, 2003. The enduring tale of literature's most famous orphan and his misadventures with a band of London boy thieves and their rascally leader Fagin, his peril at the hands of the evil Bill Sikes, and his salvation by the kindness of Mr. Brownlow.

Thomas Hardy, *Far From the Madding Crowd*. New York: Modern Library Classics, 2001. This 1874 tale of love, hope, and social class in southwest England is considered to be Hardy's first great novel. It follows the fortunes of the strong-willed Bathsheba Everdene and three very different men who love her.

William Makepeace Thackeray, *Vanity Fair*. New York: Penguin Classics, 2001. Driven by a relentless ambition, the calculating Becky Sharp strives to overcome her poor background and climb the social ladder of early–nineteenth-century London. First published in 1848, this satirical novel is thought to be Thackeray's masterpiece.

Nonfiction Books

Rupert Christiansen, *The Victorian Visitors: Culture Shock in Nineteenth-Century Britain*. New York: Grove, 2000. Christiansen takes a different approach to the subject by recounting the experiences and reactions of visiting foreigners such as American essayist Ralph Waldo Emerson, German composer Richard Wagner, and French painter Theodore Gericault.

Melinda Corey and George Ochoa, *The Encyclopedia of the Victorian World*. New York: Henry Holt, 1996. A handy reference work that indexes the people, places, politics, inventions, military campaigns, and cultural activities of the Victorian period not only in Britain but also in the United States, France, Germany, and other nations.

Carolly Erickson, *Her Little Majesty: The Life of Queen Victoria*. London: Robson, 1997. A very readable biography of Victoria, written with a strong sense of drama and detail. Recommended for both young adult and adult readers.

Dorothy Marshall, *The Life and Times of Victoria*. New York: Shooting Star, 1995. This is a well-researched, well-written account of the queen and her age. The author describes the political and social climate of the day as well as the more personal side of Victoria's life. Illustrated with paintings and engravings.

Philip Steele, *Clothes and Crafts in Victorian Times*. Parsippany, NJ: Dillon, 1998. While this book is aimed at younger readers, its appeal is broader. Lavishly illustrated with color photos and drawings, and black-and-white engravings and cartoons, it gives a concise view of the way people of the era dressed, decorated their homes, and made their crafts.

Web Sites

1876 Victorian England Revisited (www. logicmgmt.com./1876/intro.htm). A self-described "journey in time," this Web site shows how a typical middle-class Victorian family lived, decorated their home, entertained, played, and celebrated a traditional Victorian Christmas. Contents include "The Family Gallery," "Victorian Etiquette," "Fun and Games," and "A Typical Day."

Britain Express, The Victorian Period: Daily Life in Victorian England (www. britainexpress.com/History/Victorian index.htm). This basic overview of the subject includes Web pages on topics such as "The Young Queen," "The Corn Laws," "Victorian Railways," and "The Late Victorian Age," as well as "Victorian London."

Literature.org: The Online Literature Library, Thomas Hughes, *Tom Brown's Schooldays*. (www.literature.org/author/ hughes-thomas/tom-browns-schooldays). Hughes's classic novel of a schoolboy's experiences at Rugby, where he learns life lessons in integrity, hard work, and giving one's all to one's school. Based on Hughes's own experiences.

Masterpiece Theater: *Oliver Twist* (www. pbs.org/wgbh/masterpiece/olivertwist/ei_ downloadandout.html). This well-designed and informative Web site is based on the Dickens novel as dramatized on PBS's Masterpiece Theatre. It explores "Oliver's London," "Down and Out in Victorian London," "Who Was Dickens?" and other topics.

Victorian Social History: An Overview (www.victorianweb.org/history/sochistov. html). Part of The Victorian Web, this site offers scholarly essays under the headings "Condition of Life and Labor," "Race, Class and Gender Issues," "Education," and "Victorian Cities and Towns."

Video

Victoria and Albert, VHS, directed by John Ermin. BBC/Arts & Entertainment Network, 2001. A well-scripted and engagingly acted dramatization of the relationship of Queen Victoria and her German-born husband, Prince Albert. Primarily a family story, the program nevertheless presents interesting bits of British history in the telling.

Works Consulted

Books

Peter Ackroyd, *Dickens*. New York: Harper-Collins, 1990. An exhaustive study of the life and work of the great Victorian novelist Charles Dickens, successfully combining biography with criticism. Includes an extensive section of annotations and references.

Richard D. Altick, *Victorian People and Ideas*. New York: W.W. Norton, 1973. This self-styled "companion for the modern reader of Victorian literature" deals with the art, religion, literature, philosophy, and science of the era.

Gillian Avery, *Victorian People: In Life and Literature*. New York: Holt, Rinehart and Winston, 1970. This is a readable and enjoyable view of the lives and lifestyles of Victorian-era Britons. The information is well-organized and accessible. Illustrated with engravings and cartoons from the period.

Juliet Barker, *The Brontës*. New York: St. Martin's, 1994. Using excerpts from the sisters' letters and novels, the author chronicles the personal lives and writings of Charlotte, Emily, and Anne Brontë.

Isabella Beeton, *The Book of Household Management*. 1861, Facsimile edition. New York: Farrar, Straus & Giroux, 1969. The classic book of taste and manners used by thousands of women during Victoria's era.

Nicolas Bentley, *The Victorian Scene: A Picture Book of the Period, 1837–1901*. London: George Weidenfeld & Nicolson, 1968. This is an absorbing large-format book, with a multitude of historical photographs. Bentley's lively style makes for an enjoyable text.

Winston Churchill, *My Early Life: 1874–1904*. Introduction by William Manchester, New York: Touchstone, 1996. The story of the great statesman's childhood, school days, and journalistic adventures with the British army make fascinating reading.

Hannah Cullwick, *The Diaries of Hannah Cullwick, Victorian Maidservant*, ed. Liz Stanley. New Brunswick, NJ: Rutgers University Press, 1984. Miss Cullwick's revealing diaries are earnest, terse, and crammed with valuable details on the mundane activities that made up a lower-class working woman's life.

Charles Dickens, *Hard Times*, edited and introduced by Kate Flint. London: Penguin, 2003. Originally published serially in *Household Words* and then in book form in 1854. From the fact-loving schoolmaster Mr. Gradgrind to Bounderby, the heartless businessman who marries Gradgrind's daughter, to the free thinking Sissy Jupe, *Hard Times* explores the way the lives of Victorians are altered by the good and bad effects of industrialization

———, *Selected Journalism, 1850– 1870*, ed. David Pascoe. London: Penguin, 1997. Over fifty nonfiction essays written by Dickens (supplemented by other writers) for two of his literary magazines, *Household Words* and *All the Year Round*. Topics covered include the workhouses, prisons, school days, working men and women, and the police beat.

Hilary Evans and Mary Evans, *The Victorians: At Home and at Work*. New York: Arco, 1973. A close-up and thoughtful examination of the customs and occupations of Victorian Britons, with emphasis on the middle classes. The material is thoroughly researched and well presented.

Judith Flanders, *Inside the Victorian Home: A Portrait of Domestic Life in Victorian England*. New York: W.W. Norton, 2004. A brand-new and welcome addition to Victorian social history. Taking a Victorian home room by room, she paints a remarkably complete picture of the life that went on within each one.

J.F.C. Harrison, *The Early Victorians, 1832–1851*. New York: Praeger, 1971. Harrison presents a scholarly view of certain aspects of the first half of the Victorian era. Features chapters on early Victorian values, poverty, prosperity, and social change. A brief but well-chosen section of illustrations is included.

———, *Late Victorian Britain, 1870–1901*. Glasgow: Fontana, 1990. A companion book to *The Early Victorians*, this volume takes a look at the final three decades of the period. It includes chapters on labor, poverty, women's issues, beliefs versus doubt, and education.

Christopher Hibbert, *Gilbert & Sullivan and Their Victorian World*. New York: American Heritage Publishing Co., 1976. With his unfailing flair for making British history come alive, Hibbert paints an engaging picture of the trials and triumphs of Victorian England's most notable musical team.

———, *The English: A Social History, 1066–1945*. New York: W.W. Norton, 1987. A well-informed, broad view of English history that remains remarkably readable throughout, by one of Britain's premier historians.

Gertrude Himmelfarb, *The Idea of Poverty: England in the Early Industrial Age*. New York: Vintage, 1985. The author addresses the sources and effects of unrelenting poverty as it relates to the Industrial Revolution.

Lee Holcombe, *Victorian Ladies at Work: Middle-Class Working Women in England and Wales, 1850–1914*. Hamden, CT: Archon, 1973. An informative study of middle-class working women in the last half of the Victorian era. The book relates the effects of advancing technology and social mores on women's labor.

Pamela Horn, *The Victorian Town Child*. Washington Square: New York University Press, 1997. An impressively in-depth study of many aspects of youthful urban dwellers—their surroundings, their diversions, their values, and their prospects.

Walter E. Houghton, *The Victorian Frame of Mind, 1830–1870*. New Haven, CT: Yale University Press, 1957. A scholarly, yet readable study of the attitudes, values, and customs of Britons in the early to middle Victorian period.

Kristine Hughes, *The Writer's Guide to Everyday Life in Regency and Victorian England: From 1811–1901*. Cincinnati: Writer's Digest, 1998. Through a simple and logical arrangement of topics and facts, Hughes conveys a remarkable amount of information on ninety years of British history and culture. Each chapter features its own bibliography.

M. Vivian Hughes, *A London Girl of the 1880s*. London: Oxford University Press, 1936. In the second of a three-volume personal account, Hughes tells her life story as a Victorian teenager and young woman with enthusiasm and humor. She shares her experiences on such topics as schooling, churchgoing, and travel.

John M. Mackenzie, ed., *The Victorian Vision: Inventing New Britain*. London: V & A, 2001. A beautifully illustrated, large-format volume containing essays and excerpts by twelve writers on different aspects of the Victorian era.

Henry Mayhew, *Selections from London Labor and the London Poor*, ed. John L. Bradley. London: Oxford University Press, 1965. A small-format hardback, this book contains excerpts from Mayhew's multivolume study of the working classes of London, assembled from hundreds of interviews with Victorian Londoners, originally published in the 1850s and 1860s.

Jeffrey Meyers, *D.H. Lawrence: A Biography*. New York: Knopf, 1990. Meyers's biography of Lawrence is a detailed and well-crafted study of the novelist's personal and professional life, with two sections of black and white photos.

Sally Mitchell, *Daily Life in Victorian England*. Westport, CT: Greenwood Press, 1996. An exhaustive look at British Victorian life in almost every imaginable aspect. Remarkably readable despite its depth, it is one of the most thorough studies of the subject in one volume.

———, *Victorian Britain: An Encyclopedia*. New York: Garland, 1998. Mitchell's companion book to *Daily Life in Victorian England* is well organized and easy to use. Its encyclopedic format makes it useful for quick reference.

Wanda F. Neff, *Victorian Working Women: An Historical and Literary Study of Women in British Industries and Professions, 1832–1850*. New York: Humanities Press, 1967. A well-researched and clearly-written survey of the role of British women in the Victorian workforce. Includes informative charts and graphs.

Christabel S. Orwin and Edith H. Whetham, *History of British Agriculture, 1846–1914*. London: Archon, 1964. Another scholarly but nonetheless accessible survey of England's crop and livestock farming during the second half of the Victorian period. Includes a helpful chapter on landlord and tenant relations.

Ronald Pearsall, *Victorian Popular Music*. Detroit, MI: Gale Research, 1973. A fully illustrated survey of the most-loved music forms of the era. The author takes an all-encompassing look at popular songs, dances, singers, music halls, song and supper rooms, burlesque, and Victorian interest in the classical musical.

C.O. Peel, *A Hundred Wonderful Years, 1820–1920: Social Domestic Life of a Century*. New York: Dodd, Mead, 1927. This account by a Victorian woman is rich in anecdotal information about the culture, manners, and activities of the upper class.

M. Jeanne Peterson, *The Medical Profession in Mid-Victorian London*. Berkeley: University of California Press, 1978. The author profiles the state of the English medical profession from the 1850s to the 1870s, including background on the field before the Medical Act of 1858.

Charles Petrie, *The Victorians*. London: Eyre & Spottiswoode, 1960. Author and historian Charles Petrie's broad but nicely balanced view of the Britons of Queen Victoria's reign.

Daniel Pool, *What Jane Austen Ate and Charles Dickens Knew: From Fox Hunting to Whist—the Facts of Daily Life in Nineteenth-Century England*. New York: Touchstone, 1993. A highly readable survey of the day-to-day doings of Britons of the 1800s, keyed generally to the literature of the period. Includes an extensive glossary of Victorian terms.

J.B. Priestley, *Victoria's Heyday*. New York: Harper & Row, 1972. This fully illustrated study of England during the years 1850–1859 examines the topics of work, religion, morality, literature, and politics during that limited period.

W.J. Reader, *Victorian England*. London: B.T. Batsford, 1964. An intriguing and enlightening general study of the era. In a voice both readable and authoritative, Reader covers such topics as politics, public health and housing, recreation, and education.

Clarice Swisher, ed. *Victorian England*. San Diego, CA: Greenhaven Press, 2000. An excellent collection of excerpts from the works of various scholars on all facets of Victorian life. Features chapters on the rise of the middle class, changing technology, health and medicine, child labor, and many more.

Laura Wilson, *Daily Life in a Victorian House*. Washington, DC: The Preservation Press, 1993. Designed in a picture-book format, this handsome volume is accessible to all ages. Generously illustrated, the book looks not only at the functions of a Victorian house but also at the daily needs, chores, and activities of a typical Victorian family.

Esme Wingfield-Stratford, *Those Earnest Victorians*. New York: William Morrow, 1930. This is a lively examination of middle-class Britons across the central four decades of the Victorian period. It puts emphasis on morality, love, character, and spirituality.

Gordon Winter, *Past Positive: London's Social History Recorded in Photographs*. London: Chatto & Windus, 1971. To the interesting collection of pictures of Victorian life at all levels, this large-format book adds a matching selection of brief essays and extensive quotations by everyday Victorians.

Mary Ann Witt et al., *The Humanities: Cultural Roots and Continuities*, 2nd ed., vol. 2, *The Humanities and the Modern World*. Boston: Houghton Mifflin, 1985. A collection of scholarly essays on the culture and customs of the nineteenth and early twentieth centuries.

Internet Sources

Lawrence H. Officer, "Comparing the Power of Money in Great Britain from 1264 to 2002," Economic History Services, 2004. www.eh.net/hmit/ppowerbp.

David Parlett, "Parlett's Historic Card Games," Historic Card Games. www.davidparlett. co.uk/histocs.

Nicole Roth, "The Sun Never Sets on the British Empire," Virginia Tech, Department of English. http://athena.english.vt. edu/~jmooney/3044main/syllabus.html.

William Wordsworth, *The Excursion*, bk. 9, lines 294–95. www.bartleby.com/145/ww 406.html.

Index

Picture Credits

About the Author

Duane C. Damon is the author of six books and over forty articles on U.S. and world history for young readers. His work has explored such subjects as the American Revolution, the Civil War, the Old West, the Great Depression, and Nazi Germany. A Florida resident, he has a son, Drew, and a daughter, Sarah. His previous book for Lucent was *Mein Kampf: Hitler's Blueprint for Aryan Supremacy*.